The G20 t

I promise to pay the aforeme................................. ....oney lies in Wonderland where laundering rubberstamped and papered notes through taxation systems is only potentially criminal.

Sign here

Contaging

● Anthony Crawford

Author of *Identity Theft Protection* and *The Perfect Sting*

Published by

MELROSE BOOKS

An Imprint of Melrose Press Limited
St Thomas Place, Ely
Cambridgeshire
CB7 4GG, UK
www.melrosebooks.com

FIRST EDITION

Editor: Jeremy Dronfield
Cover designed by Tonya Crawford
Illustrations by Anthony Crawford
News copyrights:
   Copyright Guardian News & Media Ltd 2008
   Copyright Sun Media Feb. 2007
   Copyright Globe & Mail 2011
Photograph refs: CHTV Debt Dilemma *The Perfect Sting*, TVCogeco Your Vote 2006

ISBN 978 1 907732 00 3

Printed and bound in Great Britain by:
CPI Antony Rowe. Chippenham, Wiltshire

Contaging

The G20 Tax Invaders Plan

Anthony Crawford

Toxic Loan Approved

Targets swimming in debt saving to retire

Background and Inspiration for the Story

Tony Crawford, co-inventor of IBM JAD (Joint Application Design) and author of *The Perfect Sting* and *Identity Theft Protection*, writes a sequel learned from sleazy bankers and crafty lawyers playing games with 'Signature-Specific-Identity-Theft' geared to fool judges and make 'Doing God's Work' lawful in 'The G20 Tax Invaders Plan'.

Crawford tells a story about so-called 'Sitting Duck' tax credit saving loan accounts behind tax-sheltered financial instruments that can't be sold, or defraud without them. A bank is focused on making money make sense while tax-savers are duped into 'Making Sense Fake Money' by signing worthless paper called non-bank notes that third parties monetize – launder – for cash through taxation systems.

A shadow economy game master is the very model of a modern major general accountant overseeing people into debt with a shadow bank selling toxic loans that generate losses to claim government income tax credits.

Confusion reigns as politicians insist on paying billions to banks on one hand, while slashing government services and raising taxes on the other. Authorities refuse to regulate non-bank notes that continue to cheat taxpayers. And, they turn a blind eye to bankers using 'Bombersuits' that rely on bank agents notarizing signature affidavits to set up and collect undisclosed unsigned loans by summary judgments.

Similar to a 'Jackson Settlement' paying enormous claims all the while denying wrongdoing, a 'Bombersuit' litigates to collect questionable forged promissory notes filled out by a bank that constantly denies 'tied loans' behind potentially criminal story-book sleazy tax shelter schemes.

In this story anything goes for profit, including lawyers interfering with court documents, and perjury to obstruct justice for a bank to collect its note. The hapless defendant struggles with heavy handed lawyering that apparently continues with extortion by the bank and its agent demanding a Motion for Particulars to avoid a trial about mortgage credit default swaps sold in financial markets.

After ten years, nine judges find no credible evidence for trial with respect to bank so-called 'Sitting Duck' loans. The government decides to criminalize identity theft and politicians launching Petition 44 for an investigation into the largest bankruptcy of a financial conduit ever reported in Canada. The Minister of Finance says banks are blameless, but promises to discuss the 'Reverse Onus Rule' at the next G20…

*With opposing laws that actually
contradict professed business ethics,
it's obvious banks don't have to take
voluntary guidelines too seriously...*

THE G20 TAX INVADERS PLAN

Written in dedication to my wonderful wife Jill in memory
of a life lost in fear of a bank and its lawyers.

Also, with my special thanks to my friends in politics, Hons.
Howard Hampton and Jack Layton behind www.petition44.
com and Hon. James Flaherty for his promise to table the
'Reverse Onus Rule' for discussion at the next G20.

And lawyers without whom the story is beyond belief, and
The Tax Invaders Plan is legal and never tried.

Leader/Chef
Ontario New Democratic Party/Néo-Démocrates de l'Ontario

December, 2007

Dear Mr. Crawford,

Thank you for the information you sent me regarding Identity Theft Protection.

As you may know, consumer protection is an important issue for Ontario's New Democrats. I appreciate that you shared your book and playing cards with me.

Please be assured that we will keep up the fight to ensure Ontarians are better protected against identity theft.

Sincerely,

Howard Hampton, MPP
Leader, Ontario New Democratic Party

⊕ △···

I note the difficulties you have experienced with your dealings with the Bank of Montreal, and I have a copy of your letter from the OSC. I trust your file will be reviewed, as you have requested, and, where possible, measures taken to afford better consumer protection to you and others who find themselves in similar situations.

Sincerely, Bonnie Brown, MP Oakville.
June 16, 2005   ***Liberal Party of Canada.***

The Financial Consumer Agency of Canada does <u>not</u> have jurisdiction over contractual matters, or the general service standards of the financial institutions it regulates.

Legislation requires all federally regulated financial institutions to have in place a complaint-handling process.

Consumer concerns are important to us and we recommend you direct your complaint to the bank.

Best regards, William Knight
November 8, 2005   ***The Commissioner for FCAC.***

Ontario Legislative Assembly: NDP Petition 44 December 13, 2007.
February 26, 2009. NDP Leader Andrea Horwath Hansard Session P-44.

Disclaimer

Aside from public officials responding to complaints about bank loan procedures, including members of the 2005 Canadian Government, the Prime Minister of Canada, the Right Honorable Paul Martin, Member of Parliament, Ms Bonnie Brown, MP Oakville, and 2010 Minister of Finance, the Honorable James Flaherty, *The Perfect Sting* and *The Tax Invaders Plan* include fictional character names to fit the prose of storybook roles in sleaze and collusion to bundle bank loans with tax shelter products where the overall objective is to manufacture debt to defraud taxpayers. Any similarity to actual people and business entities is unintentional and coincidental.

This synopsis of a bank's 'no wrongdoing' lending guidelines and 'accounting scripts' refers to individuals and case law examples of banks claiming repayments of dubious loans. It includes allegations about questionable investments reported to the Ontario Securities Commission, also reviewed by the Institute of Chartered Accountants, Upper Canada Law Society, Halton Regional Police Service and the Toronto Police Fraud Squad.

The content is based on public information to create plausible reenactment with no intention to imply or infer any disregard or disrespect to any profession, or any authority mentioned herein.

A Tax Invasion Plan could be a serious matter, but this is simply... a story to raise public awareness of consumer protection issues concerning predatory lending methods including 'Identity Theft' in the design of complex financial instruments. Antiquated laws would be more easily revised if unethical business practices weren't so lucrative and dutifully rewarded.

The fiction refers to related news, talk-shows and call-in conversations. *The Perfect Sting* starts with a letter from a litigating bank that denies the possibility of unethical practices in financial institutions. The banker claims current practices are sufficient for consumer protection, and the profession is unaware of changes, or need for change, to the Canada Bank Act, or need for consumer safeguards in world markets that even after the global credit crunch continue business as usual.

This is a story that challenges the bank's assertion with a simple request that having won debt without trial they remove paid writs...

The Honourable Paul Martin, P.C., MP.
Office of the Prime Minister   June 2005

Dear Mr. Martin,

Sub: Predatory Lending Practices ~ Consumer Protection Issues
Ref: Unanswered letters from my husband over the past few years.

In follow-up to my husband's letters and appeals for assistance, I would like you to know that while the matter of this affair is the subject of a criminal investigation and professional conduct reviews: watchdog organizations appear to have no mandate for these circumstances.

As you know, from his outline of predatory lending activities, a bank used his signatures along with third party affidavits to establish an undisclosed loan in his name to participate as a partner in a tax sheltered investment scheme. The loan was disguised as a mortgage with a ten year term. It was in fact a personal debt based on and secured by a promissory note that we only became aware of after its ten year due date, when the bank sued him for its repayment.

It took years of research to gather evidence and prepare it for consideration. A decision for an investigation wouldn't have been taken lightly. Yet, in comparison, all the watchdogs we were told to contact with similar information have failed us. They refuse to recognize any wrong-doing and quickly decide it's too late to complain, and do nothing.

In the face of unanswered letters, Canada appears to be sublimely indifferent to news of US regulators battling; 'Storybook sleazy tax shelter schemes' and BBC 'Bankers Behaving Badly' in the United Kingdom.

We always thought of you as a hero because of your resolve to fight corruption. And I want you to understand that while the scam took our life savings, I also lost the husband I used to know to the ravages of a rip-off, and abuses of a bank calling him a 'Sitting Duck' in a scheme that relies on the true nature of a loan being kept secret for ten years.

I can understand the need for a 'Statute of Limitations' in many legal situations, but surely it is only a guideline to consider against the total weight of compelling evidence to follow-up a complaint.

Mr. Martin, I hope you will find it possible to influence the OSC to reopen our case file for an inquiry. And I enclose his 'bankaphobia' fantasy, which like the Gomery inquiry pays homage to, 'Oh what a tangled web we weave, when first we practice to deceive'.

He wrote it to rise above the clamor of more powerful lobbyists, and he wanted you to have it for the inevitable 'Sitting Duck' debate.

Yours very truly, Jill Crawford

Reprinted from *The Perfect Sting* by Tony Crawford © 2006

Canadian Parliamentary Review
(Legislative Report Vol 6 #1 1983[1])

Trust Companies. Late in October, it became known Cadillac-Fairview Ltd had sold nearly 11,000 apartment units in Toronto to Greymac Ltd, a Toronto trust company. This sale occasioned wide-spread concern of possible rent increases to cover the 'pass-through' of mortgage costs.

In following weeks a bizarre, confused tale unfolded, featuring rapid resale's 'flips', mysterious Saudi Arabian investors, holding companies registered in Liechtenstein, and reports that in the course of several flips, the price had escalated from $270 to over $500 million. On November 16th, Consumer and Commercial Relations Minister Dr. Robert Elgie announced a special audit of the entire transaction and introduced a bill to limit the extent to which mortgage costs from resales could be passed on to tenants in rent increases.

The Leader of the Opposition, David Peterson, and newly-elected NDP Leader Bob Rae continued to press the issue daily in Question Period, accusing the Minister of being naive in his dealings with the financiers involved and unresponsive to the needs of tenants. Controversy centered primarily on the rent implications and the adequacy of the province's rent review mechanisms.

On December 21st, the final day before the Christmas break, Dr. Elgie brought forward a bill which gave the province sweeping new powers to control and regulate trust companies. As a result of meetings with Premier William Davis and Dr. Elgie the day before, Mr. Rae and Mr. Peterson agreed to permit the bill to receive all three readings on the 21st. Little more than two weeks later, under the provisions of the new act, the province took possession of three trust companies, Greymac Trust, Crown Trust and Seaway Trust, all of which were involved in the apartment transaction. As the House resumed in mid-January the take over of these companies, the government's responsibilities for safeguarding investment in provincially-regulated loan and trust companies promised to be a hotly disputed issue for some time.

The province intervened to protect the 11,000 former Cadillac Fairview apartments from the unscrupulous gang of con-artists, Rosenberg, Markle and Player, by placing these buildings under receivership.

1   Ref: Ontario Legislative Assembly Archives – Hansard Parliamentary Session 3/L004

Bank Loan Game Rules for Sitting Ducks

In a world of corruption and endless corporate rip-offs, it's hard to avoid being victim to a clever con of one kind or another. This game involves undisclosed loans in the structure of tax sheltered retirement savings plans designed to devour private and public wealth.

The purpose of the game is making sense fake money.

The Rules:

The rules of the game are documented in a myriad of financial regulations made into laws with loopholes that allow banks and their agents to play by their own rules.

The tax shelter product is a financial instrument that has a debt repayment component such as a mortgage designed to qualify for tax credits. The government promotes the business model to encourage the general public to invest.

Banks in the game are money-lenders that underwrite tax-sheltered products sold as investments to people that sign promises to repay debt in commercial paper accepted as money thereof to pay the total cost to invest.

The Tax Invader's Plan involves two parties in a *'Step Transaction'* to manufacture debt. The first is the product provider that the investor enters the contract with. The second is a bank that sells a derivative to the main product provider that exactly matches the structured benefit of the contract. The bank represents an additional counterparty risk whereby the investors guarantee to repay any shortfall, and more important, cover any default incurred by the investment provider.

As far as the investor sees it, the agreement to pay debt to a bank is very much in the background as the legal contract, and customer contact is all with the primary provider.

The mechanics of debt creation is hidden in the contract. Once signed, the bank equates income tax credit-worthiness with personal credit for unsigned, undisclosed loans for people to borrow to invest...

The objective of the game is to sell as many tax-sheltered mortgages with as many undisclosed unsigned tied bank loans as possible to claim tax credits – it's way too easy.

Just sign here, here, and – Oh! game over, we all lose.

This storybook scheme requires an agency relationship between a bank and its product promoter to obtain signatures to defraud. The collusion is played out with serious intent for generous rewards: aside from bank promoter agents acquiring and flipping property, there is the capitalization of debt paid from private and public wealth...

The main feature of the game is known in the industry as a financial conduit that collects principal from mortgage non-bank note credit default swaps. The interest is reported to claim tax credits processed through taxation systems. The bank does the same with bank-demand notes to *'paper'* non-bank notes that can't exist or work without them.

The scheme is designed to sidestep regulations banks and developers should report in compliance. Firstly, loans and mortgages used to capitalize property are not supposed to exceed seventy-five percent of market value, and associated liens are supposed be filed with the land registry. As an investment, and as property is funded by a bank using *'structured'* financing based on investors' future income tax credits, the mortgage rule is not applicable and asset-backed securities are not reported. Secondly, as bank loans are handled by third parties that operate as bank agents, the bank does not have to contact new client-investors to confirm debt obligations. Both the bank and the product provider have a vested interest in nondisclosure behind *'Signature-Specific-Identity-Theft'*. They have no qualms selling *'Sitting Duck'* loans knowing they are risk free and legal to collect with court orders.

The trap is in *'Agency Waivers'* and *'Signature Affidavits'* witnessed by salespeople and notarized by the promoter working for the bank. In time, debtors know it's a scam but who can they call? Outside the sphere of regulatory oversight there is no protection for consumers. Judges rule *'Caveat Emptor'* in such cases: let the buyer beware...

An MP claiming expenses for a duck house makes headline news in contrast to a bank collecting a *'Sitting Duck'* loan that takes ten years and nine judges to pass judgment. Litigating one of two commingled notes while denying the other exists to avoid a trial is absurd, and a bank holding property ransom to extort release from prosecution is beyond belief. Lenders' usury tricks lead to lawyers' shenanigans and desperate efforts to quash a financial scandal that smells like a scam and blossoms with the stench of deep-rooted corruption. Enough for recipient debtors to wonder, **what the heck are non-bank notes?**

Doing God's Work…

**Lawyers, Affiants
and lenders bent
sign papered notes
tax-worthies lent,
swears to credit
heaven sent.**

Ponzi Tax Credit Savings Loan Accounts
The Perfect Pyramid for Sitting Ducks

News: Toronto Cadillac Fairview flipped $270 million apartments for $500 million in the mid-eighties would have been a nice haul if it worked. It was a simple trick by today's standards with bankers signing affidavits stating money existed where there was none. The scam started with a sworn affidavit to fake a $125 million deposit divvied up in sub-deposit affidavits for $375 million in mortgages contrived to exceed market value by about $100 million.

The purchase required bank officers to sign dozens of affidavits to account for the twenty-five percent deposit rule for second and third mortgages for real estate sales with more affidavits sent to the Land Registry to log property titles and liens.

Bankers caught red handed with signatures falsifying oaths led to criminal charges and the demises of three Trust companies that sent con-artists to jail for several months. In reflection, ingenious lenders had to devise a way to blame borrowers for being irresponsible. The solution was Ponzi tax credit default swap non-bank notes with lawyers as bank agents notarizing signature affidavits to close sales.

Oh, what a tangled web we weave,
when first we practise to deceive.

Sir Walter Scott, *Marmion*, 1808

MANUFACTURED DEBT OBLIGATIONS TO ABCP THIRD PARTY NOTES

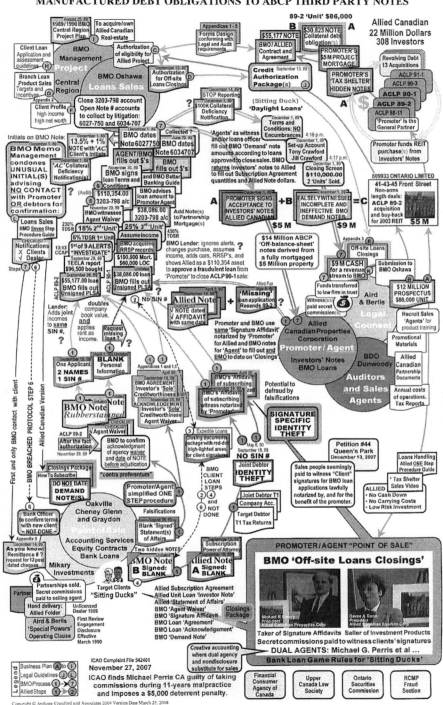

Allied Canadian ACLP 90-1 Promissory Note and BMO Loan Documents[2]

VHIS 3142 History Inquiry 3LA3 05/06/90 10:43

SUMMATION: BASED ON OUR CLIENT'S GOOD N.W @ $687M (TNW @ $536M) TDSR @ 25% WE RECOMMEND 1) EXIST CREDIT BE CONFIRMED AS IS 2) PROPOSAL OF ADD $38,086.00 ALL TACS OF ACLP90-1 //89-2 TOTAL $2963.00 -OR- 25% ALTHOUGH WIFE'S INCOME IS NOT VERIFIED FOR 1989. WE HAVE USED A MIN FIG OF $50M FOR THE YEAR FOR TDSR

Bank of Montreal — Banque de Montréal

Loan Transmittal Form
Transmission de prêt

AFFIDAVIT OF SUBSCRIBING WITNESS

I, HEATHER FERRIS , of the city of Oakville
in the Province of ___ Ontario ___ . Make oath and say:

I am subscribing witness to the attached instrument(s) and I was present and saw it/them executed at Oakville Ont by

JILL & ANTHONY CRAWFORD

I verily believe the each person whose signature I witnessed is the party of the same name referred to in the instrument.

SWORN before me at the City of)
___ Ontario ___ in the)   WITNESS
Province of ___ Ontario ___)
this 8 day of May , 19 10)
SPECIMEN SIGNATURE OF CLIENT

A COMMISSIONER FOR TAKING AFFIDAVITS

June 29 .90: 38,086

Bank of Montreal — Banque de Montréal

On demand I promise to pay to the

of Bank of Montreal
the sum of — Thirty eight thousand + eighty six — XX

and to pay interest monthly at a rate of ... per cent per annum above the Bank of Montreal's prime interest rate per annum in effect from time to time, up to and after maturity, compounded monthly from the due date of each interest until actual payment at the above mentioned branch of the Bank of Montreal. At the date of this note such prime interest rate per annum is 14.75 per cent. Value received.

Confirmation of Bank Charges
Confirmation des frais bancaires   Feb 27 , 19 91

In response to your recent request, the Bank of Montreal confirms the following Bank Charges paid during the year 19 90 .
En réponse à votre récente demande, nous confirmons par la présente, les sommes versées à titre de frais bancaires.

MR ANTHONY CRAWFORD
1761 LAKESHORE RD W
OAKVILLE
ONT L6K 1G4

351 Oshawa Main

2   Bank of Montreal Affidavit of Documents Milton Court File 1678/02

18

Rubberstamped and Papered Notes

Sully was incredulous. "We doubled it last time, and they hit him for another?" She asked her question in amazement.

"Al says he's an overpaid idiot. Always busy. He has no idea…"

"Cyn, it's a blank app!" Sully was angry. "Duh! She didn't sign it?"

"Hmmm, we only have four weeks to close. Have a word with Mykle and sort it. Tell him we'll do a note if he sends a new app with more net worth. Find out if he has an RRSP, or a company pension."

"Al says hiding notes is a cinch. People don't know what they're signing, but not loan apps, not her, especially with him in arrears already. Another app would be a dead giveaway and she's bound to ask questions." She looked Cyn in the eye. "See? That's the problem."

"If we send it back to her to sign she'll figure what his payments are for. She'll ask questions anyway. Stamp it ours to make a sale. Thirty-eight thousand isn't much. Mingle the eighty-nine and sort it later."

"Mix a ninety for her with his eighty-nine?" Sully sounded doubtful and thought of another problem. "Income? We don't have her tax return."

"Phil approved the ninety to hook L'Æmori. Cyn decided what to do. "Okay, you log she gets fifty thousand income, and I'll swap it later."

"Phew! Are you sure?"

Cyn made it so tempting. "You have her signature on his note. It's been notarized. It's your bonus. Fill it out… who's to know?"

Dear Ms. ■■■■■■

    Thank you for your letter to Mr. ■■■■ ■■■■■■*regarding a letter your office received from a constituent pertaining to* ▮▮ ■ *Financial Group's credit granting practices. As this matter falls within my area of responsibility, I welcome this opportunity to respond on our Ombudsman's behalf.*

    For the record, all credit applications and supporting documentation used for the purpose of advancing loans clearly denote the bank's logo and brand name. We are unaware of any amendments to the Bank Act governing investment loans involving third parties independent of the bank. Suffice it to say, in such situations our bank, like other financial institutions, is dedicated to uphold the highest ethical standards in all our dealings and advances funds only after performing our usual due diligence in accordance with established credit risk management guidelines. We advance credit based on the premise that we are acting on our customers' express wishes and have no reason to question their investment choices. Our approval ratios are consistent with other types of loans and are governed by the same uniform credit parameters in keeping with our decision-making processes. In the majority of cases, the customer has direct interaction with a bank employee in the finalization of their loan.

    We recognize that in any investment loan situation, there are un-certainties and potential risks and benefits associated with an applicant's investment. As with any lending scenario, we advance financing in good faith based on an assessment of the facts presented to us from a credit-granting standpoint. The bank simply acts as an independent third party lender.

    In keeping with our desire to examine and learn from feedback we receive, we would, of course, appreciate the opportunity to review the specifics of the case in hand directly with our customer and hope that your constituent gives us that chance. In the interim, thank you again for taking the time to bring this matter to our attention and for giving me the chance to provide you with some added insight from the bank's perspective.

    Sincerely yours,

    President and Chief Executive Officer

Ms. ■■■■■■■ *Legislative Assistant to Bonnie Brown MP Oakville.*
Confederation Building House of Commons Ottawa, Ontario

Toxic Loan Syndrome...

In this lending game, players as
targets are called 'Sitting Ducks'.
In litigation, as debtors, defendants
are called 'Sophisticated Investors'.

**When you understand financial miracles,
you can follow where the global credit went.
In doing God's work people wonder, *"Why so much?"***

Tony Crawford, 2010

Chapters

THE G20 TAX INVADERS PLAN
Doing God's Work

The plan of attack was in view for battle-ready troops to understand. "We are allied in greed. Your objective is to make sense fake money."

General Mo Mus spoke before a stage-wide screen: 'Toxic Loans'.

"Debt is the ultimate weapon of mass disruption. You will operate as bank agents and financial advisors saying money grows on trees." The recruits laughed at the spin. "You are trained in capitalists' bank law. You are G8 graduates with a mission to change the world order. We will be victorious in '*pincher*' maneuvers to create a global credit crunch."

The general urged his troops into battle: "You are the best graduating class yet produced and we expect you to serve Mammon beyond your wildest dreams. You will live the lives of consumers as they do. You will prey on fear of income tax and sell schemes that pay obscene bonuses to bank executives that profit from papered notes." Mo Mus looked possessed. He rubbed his hands together. "Greed is not sustainable, banks and governments will fail from tax evasion of your making. That is our tax invasion plan." He held a tight grip on the dais.

He leaned forwards to willing indoctrinated ears as the screen projected his passion in a close-up image of his rallying call. "We fight for a new world order. Fight with me," he proclaimed. "Defraud with me." His face shimmered with sweated fervor as he addressed the battalion that internalized his warmongering as their mission. "Fight with me. Paper notes for me." He beat the podium with increasing tempo.

The troops were riveted. "Stand up and fight with me." He raised his arms and lifted the air in his hands. The graduating class stood up on cue. Background music amplified a notch. ♬ "Stand up! Fight! Stand up and defraud with me," ♪ he trumpeted, just short of screeching.

An army of uniformed men and women in dress blood-red shirts and brown trousers swayed slightly as they sang in harmony. ♪ "Fight, ♪ stand up and defraud withme." ♪ The general allowed a couple of bars and then brought his hands down to pat the air for moderation.

The hall went quiet and people stood in rapt attention. "Your orders are to do battle with numbers. There's no need for the guns and knives you were trained to use before you came here." He nodded and smiled in response to grinning faces. "You are *agents provocateurs* to spread debt crises like a plague. You will be incognito for your own good. You will contage on your own for ten years until you return to base to celebrate a glorious victory of toxic loans like a contagion in decadent economies."

The graduates murmured as he continued, "There is no danger. You have an affidavit-taking-debt-creating-moneymaking machine in your arsenal for economic warfare in shadow economies. The merest whiff of its motion will corrupt. People are conditioned to trust banks police won't investigate. They wouldn't dare find fault with papered notes that launder tax credits for cash through taxation systems. It is the law, and it won't stop you."

He looked at his trained operatives who knew it to be true. They felt invincible. "Brokers will assist you. Bankers will use the courts as their collection agencies for trick loans secured by notes stamped in red. It will cause mayhem. Politicians will turn on their constituents. They will print money to bail out banks in default. They will repeal civil liberties and generations will be saddled with sovereign debt that lies in Wonderland. Countries will blame each other for economic ruin."

"Some of you will be financial advisors, others bankers. Your mission is to paper non-bank notes." He saluted. "Report back in ten years."

BANK LOAN DEPENDENT THIRD PARTY NOTES
How to Swap Witness to Bank-loan Notes that Paper Non-bank Notes

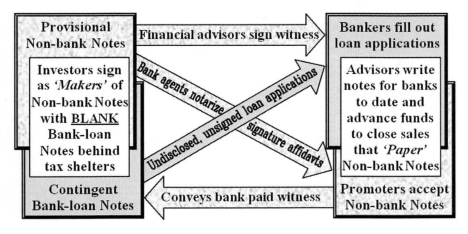

Proclamation by the Grace of Our Sharper Leader and Master of the Great Divide.

Confoundation Court Report 1678/02 and Appeal Justice Rules C49171

'Sitting Duck' Loans do <u>NOT</u> Exist.

The departments of Summary Judiciary and Bank Lore (All praise the Gallows Prosecutor and the Prime Compounder) make a joint solemn proclamation to dispel delusions promoted by followers of fashionable discontent that toxic loans cause liquidity problems in financial markets. There is no truth in rumors that banks write notes to create debt that should be regulated instead of forgiven at taxpayers' expense.

We refer to folklore emanating from the life of Robby Ducky.

It will be clear to readers the author has strayed into realms of fantasy that fails to impress even the most cynical and radical among us. A debtor's portrayal of banks conveying improperly witnessed notes they fill out to collect by litigation is clearly ridiculous.

Aspersions the Supreme Judiciary (All praise the Gallows Prosecutor) collude with lawyers to obstruct justice demonstrate sour grapes with no foundation in fact. Nine-years' litigation delivered rulings from nine judges that upon examination in four hearings found no basis in spurious arguments and allegations dismissed by honorable justices as unbelievable *Alice in Wonderland*. Indeed appeal judges confirm no wrongdoing by the MOB as the bank's lawyer persuaded the bench there are no genuine issues for trial that would not be successful.

The writer's allusion to 'Sitting Duck' loans is simply wrongheaded and disingenuous. Similarly, there are no such things as 'Red Notes' in financial markets. Nor is there any connection to recessions, or sovereign debt crises brought on by external forces from unruly and disorderly unregulated economies beyond the Great Divide.

Nor is there any connection to ABCP Third Party Notes in the largest 32 billion bankruptcy of a financial conduit in Confoundation history.

Supposed impacts of 'Sitting Duck' loans and 'Red Notes' differ from conformist aspirations of the Eminent Overseer. (All praise the Chief Proctor.) No self-respecting Confoundation (Hail our Sharper Leader) would ever allow itself to be consumed by plainly obvious corporate efforts to deprive loyal citizens of hard earned wealth and happiness.

The idea of a 'debt-creating-affidavit-taking-money-making machine' to steal income tax credits that investment bankers and brokers swap for cash from the public purse is sheer lunacy. Obviously, the writer's evil rhymes are trumped-up ravings of a fractured mind.

Our consent to publish a confession from the Fouter Central Agency for Collections (All praise the Gallows Prosecutor) is to bring a wayward author to his senses after humiliating failures, poor reviews, and broad rejection by well-balanced judges. He will learn he surpassed the limits of fervent imaginings. On reflection of favors for release he will be encouraged to more stable and constructive endeavors.

Also, the Confoundation (Hail our Sharper Leader) does not want to appear despotic and is quite certain reading this volume will confirm how misguided and futile it is to mock confounded rules and time tested convention for economic stability, law, and order. (All praise the High Chancellor, the Supreme Prosecutor, and the Chief Proctor.)

From illustrious offices of the very highest placed authorities in the Confoundation, I assure the United People of the Great Divide that we have studied the facts and unreservedly and in conclusion hereby state: ***SITTING DUCK LOANS AND RED NOTES DO NOT EXIST***.

There is no case for intervener status. Debt to the MOB is a personal problem for the likes of Robby Ducky. The matter is closed and this is definitely the last word from the supreme legislative assembly.

Lurid Bison Ceboid,

Deputy Minister for the Gallows Prosecutor
Most Omnipotent Sharper Leader
and Master of the Great Divide.

Most Majestic Mastiff Badio Dinwuddy
Summary Judiciary of the Confoundation and Great Divide
and Master Fouter of the Central Agency for Collections
(All praise the Gallows Prosecutor).

Your Most Majestic Mastiff

I, Robby Ducky, in all humility and gratefulness for the honor to write you, do herewith bestow myself upon your splendid and sympathetic leniency, and extend my pleadings with utmost courtesy as follows:

In return for alluded compassions and stereotypical forgivenesses oft-times extended to iniquitous types in the Confoundation, I take upon myself, as directed, to make a full record of my lapses from propriety. I regret it will be a convoluted story as I have to inform you that my sins, albeit creative, encompass treachery and contemptible disrespect of general accounting principles. Violations include almost every diktat and edict in the Confoundation Act of Naissance. I confess to being a conniving if not convivial scoundrel. Your Mastiff was most sage and prudent to have me incarcerated immediately on hasty judgment by the Supreme Judiciary (All praise the Gallows Prosecutor).

Therefore I discontinue litigation in gratitude for gracious allowances such as splints for my fingers that I may hold a pen, and transferring me to a cabal with high windows for enlightenment to write on paper generously provided for retractions that in truth are supported with letters and pictures and indeed court records of despicable acts.

On reflection of constant questioning and guilt-wracked tormented soliloquy and knowing your interest in Mykle L'Æmori as champion of growth and prosperity in loony markets, I confess to converting non-bank notes to money from empty promises given currency in his name signed in acceptance thereof. In this, I am guilty as charged of looting public coffers by heinous tax evasion and wicked crimes against the Confoundation and trusting people of the Great Divide.

It is by accident of birth and karma that my frailties lean to the wrong side of Confoundation law. I beg indulgences and leniencies in consideration of misfortunes that befall people with little choice of fate and unseen forces that direct poor miserable lives. It cannot be helped that cheating comes in the basic nature of a wretch like me.

So, as judged, I compare my meanderings to *Alice in Wonderland*.

While writing confessions to gain special treatments and tremendous dispensations, my mind takes leave to a rabbit hole in a make-believe world, forsooth like Alice, that the Confoundation might condescend to a teeny little trial. (Hail our Sharper Leader. And all praise the Shadow Chancellor, the Supreme Prosecutor, and the Chief Proctor.) To wit:

*Alice, **"If I had a world of my own, everything would be nonsense. Nothing would be what it is, because everything would be what it isn't. And, contrary wise, what it is, it wouldn't be, and what it wouldn't be, it would. You see?"***

Lewis Carroll ~ *Alice in Wonderland.*

I should not have made non-bank notes with exaggerated claims that money lies in Wonderland. The court could not have known, indeed, and no doubt, the Confoundation did <u>not</u> know it would be easy for 'Makers' to create cash out of thin air by which 'Holders' launder tax credits as money from the Shadow Chancellor.

I am found bound in debt to undisclosed loans by signature affidavits notarized by the honorable Mykle L'Æmori. By your leave, public awareness of 'Signature-Specific-Identity-Theft' will alert con artists to banks that take liberties with people's financial and personal information in order to set up bogus tax credit savings loan accounts.

A fool and his money are soon parted, and it is with abject apologies I present a sorry tail of malfeasance motivated by lust for loonies.

Yours with due respect and humbleness, and forever in your debt,

R Ducky

ABCP Debt Wish

"You can go in now."

Sully, Bræn and Cyn stood up together like synchronized puppets on a string. Cyn fiddled his tie and nudged it to a slight angle, he had no idea if it was straight or not. A smartly dressed secretary smiled and opened a highly polished door that ended the executive wait game.

"Sully VanScrawl, Bræn Chyld, Cyn Fordo to see you sir." The lanky lady closed the door leaving them facing the president of the MOB.

People in finance know Phil Morrsacs from his presidential image in bank journals. He rose from a well-padded deeply dimpled executive swivel chair behind a massive burnished desk in oak and fine leather inlay. He looked exactly like his picture, wearing a dark blue pinstripe suit, a light blue shirt with a white collar and a navy blue tie.

"I'm Phil," he said holding out a hand in greeting. "Sully, good to see you." He continued clasping hands that reached out to his. "You must be Bræn Chyld from Lemons Broth." He shook the offered hand vigorously. "Hey Cyn." He held Cyn's hand in a firm grip and steered him round a conference table to a high corner view of the city waterfront. "You've been with us, mmm, how long now?" he murmured.

"Thirteen years, from Queen's '75," Cyn blurted but he relaxed as they admired the view of the lake. Phil rested his arm on a highchair.

"How did the move to Osowega go? Settled in? Good school?"

"Oh yes, great, we love it." Cyn glowed. "The town's expanding and there's more and more people moving in. It's a nice neighborhood, the branch is in a good location and business is growing all the time."

"Good to hear, good to hear. Bræn, you're new to the MOB, eh?"

"Yes sir, I was at risk with Bare Stones before I sold Lemons."

"Good banks, we need your experience. They tell me you have ideas about closing loans, so let's hear about it." Phil turned and pulled out a chair and sat with his back to the window. "Take a pew," he invited.

Bræn stood near to the president's right, but Cyn took a seat to the left and Bræn decided to sit next to him. He strode round as the door opened and the lady from reception brought a tray with cups, a flask of coffee, sugars, creamers, and dark chocolate-coated digestive biscuits.

Bræn and Sully sat down as the president's personal assistant set the table and said, "Geosh is on his way, sir."

"Geosh Ozegle is MOB law," Phil smiled and looked at Cyn. "I want his opinion about this 'Off-site Loans Closings' idea of yours."

"Well, it's really Bræn's idea, he knows the details." Cyn hedged and said, "We've a lot of wealthy clients who need financial advice. This is about people owning commercial property. It's a tax shelter deal that charges interest on investment loans to claim credits. It's good business for Investment Banking and Wealth Management Services, but there's profit in retail if we underwrite deals to buy real estate."

"Do you have one in mind?"

"Yes sir, it's a project. Mykle L'Æmori owns a commercial building downtown. He used to be a lawyer with Ardent Bailiffs and he wants us to underwrite it for a tax shelter."

There was a knock on the door and a thin smartly dressed wiry man walked in with a manila folder held close to his chest. "Phil," he nodded and sat down to the right of the president, who introduced him.

"Geosh Ozegle, meet Bræn Chyld, Cyn Fordo and Sully VanScrawl."

"Right," Geosh said, "we met on the phone. I've looked into it."

"Good," Phil said looking round. "We're just starting with Cyn."

"Yes." Cyn swallowed to relieve his dry throat. "Here's a picture." He felt a bit choked and wanted a drink, but no one touched the coffee.

Bræn chipped in: "We reckon about twenty million loonies from the Confoundation. It's a bluebird," he said with a wink and a smile that changed to a smirk. He leered as he spread prints of an old building with store frontage and large signage 'Mounting Gear' on the table.

They looked at the pictures. "Location," Phil said approvingly.

"Yes." Cyn recovered his voice. "As I say, a lawyer bought it for about four million. He mortgaged it for five with rent guarantees taken from income that investors claim as losses for income tax credits."

"Is it ours already?" Phil probed as he looked at the picture.

"Sunny Loaf has the lien," Cyn answered and paused. "L'Æmori knows the game. He has a ten million note on it selling two hundred units at seventy-five thousand. He rakes five million from investors' notes at twenty-five thousand a unit to cover the mortgage. We get ten back from fifty thousand tax credits in personal loans. Here's the deal." Cyn placed a magenta brochure on the table.

Phil had been an investment banker before the MOB and he summed up. "He holds a five million loony mortgage on property that's worth four million that we sell for ten to people taking out personal loans. Right? Investors claim tax credits for the interest they pay to us."

"Yes sir, at fourteen percent." Cyn noticed Phil raise an eyebrow.

"Four times negative equity," Phil observed. "Who appraised it?"

"Badio Dinwuddy." Cyn pointed to an office tower east of the MOB.

"Ah, the friendly frauditors." He encouraged Cyn to continue: "Go on."

"Right, here's the plan…" Cyn was more confident: "L'Æmori sets up five million in investors' notes to resell the mortgage and we lend ten million in equity loans to qualified investors who want to buy it."

"Why risk ten on negative equity?" Phil waved at the picture.

"We don't. We assess clients' equity for loans based on investors' net worth and creditworthiness. L'Æmori documents debt to third party notes and we secure personal loans with demand notes."

Phil returned a knowing smile to Geosh's almost imperceptible nod.

"It's going to be a hard sell if punters spot two notes in the deal."

"Easy if they don't," Geosh responded with a gaze to make a point.

Phil looked at Geosh a moment longer. "Ah, right, I'm hooked, tell me how it works." He looked at Bræn and to Cyn for the answer.

"Well first," Cyn extended the first finger of his left hand and pinched it between a thumb and forefinger of his right, "L'Æmori bundles our notes with investment agreements which are loan apps." He paused.

"Second," he said, holding his second finger, "investors sign contracts, promissory notes, our waivers, affidavits, and loan apps at red dots, leaving everything blank, especially MOB notes." He paused again.

Cyn moved his pincer grip to his third finger. "Third, L'Æmori is a lawyer willing to notarize bank 'Affidavits of Subscribing Witness' to identify people's signatures that make demand notes legally binding."

He held his pinky finger and jiggled it to make the point. "We fill out our notes in credit amounts we approve for investors to afford to buy units. Then we set up daylight loans to close sales to pay L'Æmori who fills out his notes for units sold, mm?" He looked over his hand.

As Cyn ran out of digits he extended an open palm and slapped it with his first two fingers to make a point. "We swap L'Æmori's notarized witness from his notes to our notes as if witnessed by Kaleidoscope sales reps," he said triumphantly. He snapped his hand shut to grasp paired forefingers in a fist that he shook to demonstrate entrapment.

5.3 Duty to Investors

*The developer or promoter of a real estate or other type of investment scheme will invariably have an established relationship with one or more financial institutions. **A common scenario is where individual investors are given pre-printed loan applications from that financial institution at the time of purchase.***

The loan documents will generally clarify that each loan decision is being made based on the creditworthiness of the individual investor independently of the agreement between the investor and developer, or promoter. *The financial institution is making no representation as to the merit of the investment scheme, and owes no fiduciary duty to the investor. At the time, the Offering Memorandum ('OM') for the investment opportunity usually expressly excludes the bank from any liability for any misrepresentations in the OM.*

Despite these obstacles, investors have often tried to escape their liability under such loans by claiming breach of fiduciary duty by the financial institutions. The onus is on the investors to demonstrate the existence of a fiduciary relationship. The claim will generally fail, particularly where:

1. The financial institution is not a party to the main agreement.

2. The financial institution does not in any way participate in the marketing or promotion of the venture, including the preparation and distribution of the promotional material, nor is it mentioned in any of the promotional material.

3. Obtaining financing from the financial institution is not a mandatory or integral part of the transaction.

4. There is little or no direct contact of any sort between the investors and representatives of the financial institution.

5. In addition to being educated and sophisticated in their own right, each investor is at liberty to obtain independent legal advice.

However, where a potential investor made personal contact with the financial institution to obtain advice regarding the investment and advice was given, there may be an issue as to whether the financial institution owed a duty of care to the investor to advise him or her of exactly what investigation the financial institution has done of the investment structure or to warn that the financial institution was not promoting the investment and that they should make their own decision to seek independent advice:

(Abstract from) **Fiduciary Duties** *(2004 – Rel.1)*

Phil followed but needed clarification. He turned to Geosh. "Sounds like we fill out notes to secure undisclosed loans for people to borrow to buy what we underwrite. How do you make it legal?" It was a very important question, and he wanted to hear the answer from Geosh.

"Dealers handle off-site loans when people finance purchases such as cars. This way, people sign blank notes and we approve loans to close sales. We need borrowers' authorizations and agency waivers, dealers have to notarize clients' signatures so they don't have to sign loan applications. All we do is fill out notes for how much credit we think they can afford to invest. They have no idea we exist." Geosh paused and opened his folder for a handout. "We rubberstamp blank notes," he explained briefly as he laid down the law.

Geosh knew they wouldn't read it, but it was his duty to the president to be frank. Phil had to know the rules to gamble people's money.

He said, "There are some risks and we have to make sure we're safe on points of law. Sales are dependent on loans so nondisclosure is a given. Dealers can't disclose business relationships with banks, any more than we can reveal relationships with promoters as agents. We are talking investors making notes that brokers fill out and accept as money to close sales. The note terms are derived from the mortgage. We can't acknowledge or include investors' debt when we adjudicate their personal credit for equity loans. Reps explain the mortgage but they don't tell people about loans to borrow to invest so we can't advise terms and conditions until after closings. It's tricky. Neither of us complies with bank regulations." He shrugged. "Our loan decisions establish secondary risk, so we need waivers and acknowledgements and the broker has to notarize signature affidavits to identify debtors."

"Have you got it covered?" Phil asked a question that made Bræn's heart sing. Cyn and Sully stared intently at Geosh with anticipation.

"Well, we have laws 2, 4 and 5." Geosh pointed to the boilerplate.

Geosh took a breath. "We're most exposed on 1 and 3." He read the law: "*The financial institution is not a party to the main agreement... Obtaining financing from the financial institution is not a mandatory or integral part of the transaction.* We have to be careful people don't find out they make non-bank notes that depend on bank transactions." He let it sink in. "We convert tax credits into debt." He was blunt and he looked for reaction. Only Phil seemed interested in the law.

"Our loans start with provisional agreements that brokers lend money to people signing notes to be paid with cash from investments. Bank loans buy investment property but we need to confirm investors sign their notes before we make ours. Investors' notes are worthless until they're papered with bank loans to add loonies to the deal for brokers to accept as IOUs. We both hold notes after closings. You see?"

Phil rubbed his chin. "Don't they have to be witnessed to be legal?"

"Our notes are signed blank. They're rubberstamped and filled out and we date them to close sales. Technically, they're not witnessed."

Phil got the idea. Still holding his chin, he rolled his head to an angle to look at the clever Bræn. "Done these before?" he quizzed.

Bræn smiled and said, "Yes sir. The witnessing we're talking about is an 'Affidavit of Subscribing Witness' in the package to be signed by investors and witnessed by sales reps and notarized by the broker at the time of sale." He handed out a business concept chart knowing he would have to explain it in simple terms. Even to savvy bankers.

Cyn described how to swap witness. "The purchase price of the tax shelter is the sum of two loans secured by two notes on the left. Paid witness to non-bank notes is transferred to bank-demand notes on the right that we fill out to advance money to people borrowing to invest. Our loans fund closings when the promoter signs acceptance of non-bank notes as real money papered from personal loans to the financial instrument, which in this case is L'Æmori's mortgage derivative."

BANK LOAN DEPENDENT THIRD PARTY NOTES
How to Transfer Witness to Bank Notes that Paper Non-bank Notes

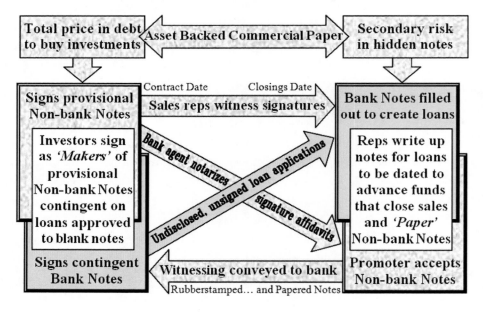

Bræn demonstrated his experience using process charts to transfer knowledge. He felt ready to continue with a more detailed chart.

"Tax," Bræn said. "When I worked for Lemons we invented ABCP – Asset Backed Commercial Paper – to capitalize negative equity. It's all about SIVs – Structured Investment Vehicles designed to hold assets with the sole purpose of making tax credit claims against them."

"Our long term goal is to acquire property." It was very important Phil bought the scam. Bræn wondered how to frame it for Geosh to agree to leverage a loophole in Confoundation law.

"It's a step transaction."

In a flash of brilliance Bræn reached for the sugar bowl and nudged it to Phil Morrsacs. "Think of this as a financial conduit point-of-sale, and these packages are notes and signature affidavits," he said.

Bræn selected two red sweeteners and a blue sugar. "People create money out of thin air when they sign banknotes." He grinned as he watched bankers nod in silent agreement. He arranged red-blue-red packages slanting the chart. "Red Note A secures the promoter's loan and Red Note B is our loan we approve to close the sale amount.

We need a rep to witness signing and the bank agent has to notarize it on the blue affidavit in the middle to identify who signed both notes."

Everyone was fascinated by the demonstration as Bræn droned, "The first red note is debt owed to the promoter paid by an investment that can't exist until we decide how much an investor can afford that we fill out on a banknote to paper debt to a non-bank note." He pointed to the second red. "We open an account to advance borrowed money to the promoter." He pointed to the first red sachet and picked it up and punched it in the air. "The dealer gets the investor's note back to fill out the number of units sold from our credit decision," he grinned.

Bræn jiggled the red sachet in his hand. "Non-bank notes go back to Kaleidoscope as debt to loonies." He dropped it in the sugar bowl and nodded at the remaining blue and red sachets. "You see what's left, a blue witness to a red note. It's all we need to create and collect debt." He leaned back and looked expectant, as if he deserved applause.

Phil looked at Bræn and noted Sully and Cyn smiling. Three wired bankers waited for a decision from the president to do God's work.

"Well Geosh, do we have a package for the job?" he quipped.

"With the right legalese. But it would be tricky if it ever got to trial."

Phil accepted the notion. "What are the chances of that?"

41

'OFF-SITE LOANS CLOSINGS' STEP TRANSACTION
Manufactured Debt Obligations to Rubberstamped and Papered Notes

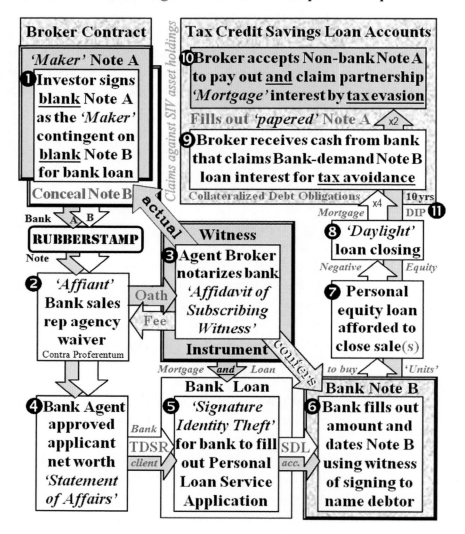

"When we swap L'Æmori's notarized witness from non-bank notes to bank-demand notes to identify people, they can't deny they signed notes or waivers. Judges call them debtors so the courts work for us as collectors." Geosh smiled. "We get summary judgments to avoid trials to explain the setup. We can't lose. It's our law, we write it."

"Right, good… who fills out MOB notes?" Phil asked with a smile.

Cyn looked at Sully, and she grinned. "I do," she gushed. "Reps do it. Gee, there'll be so many. I guess we'll all do it." They laughed.

Phil smiled and reached out for a cup and saucer and poured himself a coffee. He stood up and carried it to the window and looked out while the others took the presidential cue to imbibe.

They gathered in the corner view of the lake, staring out as tourists might from high towers. Phil drank his coffee and returned his cup to the table. He looked at Bræn's chart again and pointed the first box under the words 'Broker Contract' to ask Geosh a question.

"Geosh, how do we get tax savers to make non-bank notes?"

Geosh considered the trick and recited from years of bank legalese without hesitation, "FOR VALUE RECEIVED, the undersigned (herein called the 'Maker') promises to pay…" Geosh tightened his lips and nodded, confirming. "Yes, that'd do it. With power of attorney thrown in for good measure." He looked a bit wistful in contemplation.

Phil pondered the tax components shown as business outcomes for revenue. "So investors claim tax credits on notes A and B?"

"Ours are legit for tax," Geosh held; "we fill out bank-demand notes to set up loans for people to pay interest on them for tax credits. Non-bank notes are genuine in as much as people sign to make debt to claim tax credits. Promoters accept debt to non-bank notes as money to collect interest from the investment to pay the mortgage. Investors don't actually pay the interest. It's just a way of accounting for them to claim losses for tax credits. It continues until the property is sold, when the promoter cashes debt to non-bank notes. If the original asset, the investment property, increases enough to pay out bank-demand notes they're none the wiser. The best they can do is break even."

"Fat chance at four times negative equity, eh?" Phil observed wryly.

"Hmmha," Geosh chuckled. "People don't realize how much we want their signatures for tax credits when they make notes. They complain when we tell them how much debt they made in fake money."

"That's what we're here for, our shareholders expect it," Phil mused presidentially. He shook the plan in his hand to stay on topic. "But they still report interest on both notes for personal tax credits?"

"Oh yes, they certainly do that." Geosh wondered where Phil was going with the conversation.

"So there is tax evasion, I mean, if anyone got really anal about us stamping signed notes, we could send them to jail for tax evasion?"

Geosh wasn't known to josh, but he choked and blurted, "That's rich, we rubber-stamp notes to collect people's tax credits, and they go to jail." His eyes bulged as he trembled with joy just thinking about it. "Wow, what fun in Chambers! The bench will love judging these."

Bræn was quietly congratulating himself, noting maliciousness creep into the plan. Phil poured another coffee and rejoined the group.

Phil turned. "Right Bræn," he said, "I like the way you think. You will do well here." He looked puzzled. "Tell me, what's the SDL arrow?"

Bræn realized that Phil didn't miss much as he explained the acronym. "It's jargon, SDLs are 'Sitting Duck Loans' for namesake debtors."

It was a new one to Phil and it amused him. He thought of SDLs and ABCPs and chuckled. "Harrumph! We'll be Sully's ABCP team."

Everyone smiled as Phil sipped coffee and snorted as he did a name roll call pointing with his saucer from man to man. "We're Sully's ABCP team. He looked thoughtful. "Geosh I want you to fix L'Æmori up with a contract as the team leader. Bræn, I want a step transaction checklist for 'Off-site Loans Closings'. And, Cyn, I want you to report MOB 'Daylight' loans as customers' savings loan accounts."

Phil grinned. "P is me, Phil's project," he lifted his cup to his lips for a sip as he pointed an extended pinky towards Sully. "S is for as many as possible." They laughed at the banker's witty banter.

Bræn raised his cup in gratitude. "ABCP," he said. "Cheers."

They all smiled, "ABCP, cheers."

Affiant Rules

"Kaleidoscope, Façade Properties," the speakerphone squawked.

"Mykle L'Æmori, please."

"Yes sir. Can I say who's calling?"

"Geosh Ozegle. MOB Law."

"Yes sir, please hold… transferring you now, go ahead sir."

"Mykle L'Æmori here."

"Yes, Mykle, it's Geosh Ozegle from MOB Corporate Law."

"Oh yes, they said you'd call, how can I help?"

"It's about the Façade deal. I need to clear a few things up before you see our people at the Osowega branch. OK?"

"Right."

"I want to make sure you understand 'Off-site Loans Closings' is a bank within a bank with the same operations. We have to make sure you follow procedures. How many people do you have in sales?"

"Hmm, we have Daveh Gumn and a secretary with four sales reps and an administrator. We pay commissions to accountants and financial advisors in the field. Can't say exactly how many, some are more successful than others. They come and go… you know how it is?"

"Well we don't want anything to go wrong, the main thing is bank documents we need. We hold you responsible to keep a tight reign. I want you to sign an agreement you will handle all the loans yourself. I'm talking as a lawyer; you know about compliance? Right?"

"No problem, I know how to handle documents." Mykle felt hot.

"Right, Bræn Chyld and Cyn Fordo will talk to you about business operations, but I'm calling you about legal matters."

Mykle assumed Geosh knew he was a lawyer. "Protocol?"

"Yes. After investors sign as 'Makers' of non-bank notes, we have to make sure the law works for us to collect, you understand?"

"Oh, right," said Mykle. "We have that covered in the first line of the investor's note, FOR VALUE RECEIVED, the undersigned (herein called the 'Maker') promises to pay… etcetera. Don't worry about legalese. I know the script. You can check it if you want."

"I will. We will check the contract, the loan package. You know we need acknowledgements and agency waivers to approve them, right?"

"Hm." Mykle indicated understanding and Geosh continued.

"Second, we need witnessed signatures. You have to notarize each affidavit yourself. Exclusive. No other takers, you *do* understand?"

Mykle thought he had better speak plainly: "Absolutely, we're talking 'Affiant Rules'. I don't pay reps unless they bring signed contracts to me, and I notarize their witnessing of client signatures for the bank."

"Right, you'll have to do more than tell them. It's very important. We have a checklist that each contract and signature affidavit is notarized by you and correctly dated before we set up any loan for a loony."

Mykle was alarmed. "I only sign as a taker of affidavits. That's all there is to it. It's hard to read my name and I won't stamp them, or track IDs. You don't need me to do that, right?" He felt exposed and sounded as firm as he could for as much as he was willing to do.

"Mmm. It'll work for us, as long as you're the only notary. Okay?"

Mykle was relieved to hear it. His arrogance returned in self-esteem. He smirked at the phone. "I'll do as many as you want."

"We'll see," Geosh said bluntly. "Now, about MOB demand notes. You have to be sure they're signed blank for closings. They can only be filled out and dated when we advance funds to you on the last day they're offered. That's how it's done. No exceptions. Is that clear?"

Finally, Mykle knuckled to authority. "Yes sir," he said.

"You'll need our help to do 'Off-site Loans Closings'. We will send people to your office to key in loans and return the rest to you to sign acceptance of investors' notes when the loonies flow."

The line was silent as it dawned on Mykle how careful he had to be with bank documents for their protection. He had to comply with protocol to set up a step transaction geared to cheat people out of tax savings. "Do you want a copy of our 'How to subscribe' guidelines?"

"Yes, I do. You have to get your sales people clear on what has to be signed." Geosh kept the upper hand, "I want to check Kaleidoscope procedures personally, if you want to be a banker you'll have to sign a MOB 'Off-site Loans Closings' agreement. Cyn will get back to me. If things work out I will want to see you at my office to go over the details. You'll have to sign a contract to join the MOB."

Geosh took Mykle's silence as agreement. "Thank you. Goodbye."

"Yes, thank you Geosh. Goodbye." Mykle put the phone down slowly. And a moment later… he rubbed his hands together…

Mykle L'Æmori thought of money, lots and lots of money, and he beamed a really big cheesy grin with greed written all over it.

Bank Loan Game Rules for Sitting Ducks

"Here's something to read."

"What is it?"

"It's a paperback, a step transaction guide for tax avoidance."

Mykle L'Æmori looked at the book and shuffled in his chair that faced the bank officer seated at a large oak desk with his name highly visible: Cyn Fordo, Osowega Branch, Executive Loans Manager, in large chrome-plated glitzy letters on black plastic with a holder for business cards and a pen on the end of a chrome ball-link chain.

"Cyn, I thought you said it was easy, that's why we're here."

The property developer looked at Cyn directly, but instead of a steady gaze for an answer, his eyes wandered to framed certificates and a scenic poster on the wall promoting high goals and achievement. He was an impressive-looking man with a stocky frame and a high, somewhat exaggerated forehead due to premature balding with a bushy mane of mousy hair over his ears, round the sides and back. His face was unblemished, babyish and featureless except for a pair of shiny clear-rimmed glasses. He was dressed smartly in light slacks with a dark jacket and a fitted pale pink shirt sporting a coordinated red tie.

Mykle was someone used to being in charge. He was quick to face Cyn squarely with a steady stare of blue eyes above a thin smile that portrayed a questioning look of superiority. It transformed to a glare of someone waiting for an answer. It put Cyn on the defensive.

"Oh well, it is… there's a lot of money involved, you know we have to be careful." Cyn sounded protective and even a bit subdued.

Cyn had looked forward to the meeting. It was underlined in his diary. Sales told him about thirty-five million loonies hinged on the meeting going well. He had thought he was ready for it.

They had met before and written each other, but Cyn hadn't expected such an awkward start in conversation. Next time he would think of a better approach than presenting a novel as surprise reading material.

Cyn began to get used to the idea it was just about loonies, pure and simple capitalism, they would behave like this for years to come.

He looked at the lady who joined the meeting. She was also dressed in business attire and looked elegant in a pleated skirt with a matching jacket in lighter tones and padded shoulders that made her look bigger than she actually was. Her blouse was detailed with bright embroidery and a striking cravat tied in a loose fluffy bow. She had dark hair and brown eyes, and her face was finely chiseled to a small round dimpled chin surrounded with downcast lines that drooped from both edges of her bottom lip under a slightly sullen beaky overbite.

There was a lull and Cyn went on, "Anyway, I put my business card in the inside cover." He looked at it and murmured, "It's a signed copy. You can read it whenever…"

The other man glanced at it, and leaned forward and pushed it aside while he looked up with a slight frown. At the same time he sluffed two business cards face up across the table with a steady hand that reached over like a card dealer in a casino. He left them for Cyn to pick up to read, Mykle L'Æmori, President, Kaleidoscope Properties Corp. And, Daveh Gumn, President, Kaleidoscope Equities Corp.

Daveh looked at Cyn as he read her business card. "I've just started, I'm in charge of investment sales and operations," she said.

Her hair was short and fashionably unkempt in tight frizzy curls styled in a boy's cut that accentuated petite ears with flecked bulbous earrings chosen to match her necktie. Cyn watched her and noticed one eyebrow was curved round and relatively still, whereas the right flattened out to a slanted corner. It was more animated and gave the effect of a one-sided expression of surprise whenever she spoke.

It preoccupied Cyn for a moment.

When the two men made eye contact, Mykle probed: "You said the MOB would front the project we talked about?"

"Oh! Yes, of course we will, Mykle." He paused to think. "We've done these before, er, tell me more about it?"

It was an open question and Cyn leaned back in his chair where his elbows found familiar recesses in worn leather armrests. He raised his fingertips to his nose and pressed his hands together in anticipation. It was a good image he thought. He remembered MOB sales training: get to know the client and let them do the talking… it tells you what you need to know. It gives you time to think and be in control.

Mykle was brief and to the point. "It's all here in a private Offering Memorandum. It's a famous old building in a good location in the business core. We've got good tenants and steady income. There's a page from an appraiser for ten million depending on the model for a ten million note, plus a five million mortgage covered with a rent guarantee. I wrote you. We want to develop it as income-producing real estate to pay out the mortgage and raise capital to acquire the property next door. It's all here." He put a folder on Cyn's desk and tapped his stubby index on a letter clipped to a glossy brochure.

Cyn looked but didn't read the letter. It was a brief of what he knew already. He folded it behind the brochure and held it from curling back. He looked at the Kaleidoscope mascot, a gold-trimmed tricorn centered in a magenta background with a picture of an elegant office below an address line in bold letters, 41-43-45 Façade, Ogstowne.

Cyn recognized it and said, "I've seen this. It's in a good location. It's the Budsmoor Building on the front near Saint Florence Market."

Mykle nodded. "We have a prospectus and Offering Memorandum, but it's not filed because each unit is less than a hundred and fifty grand. The deal closes December one, eighty-nine. We can sell with Cybecie loans, but they need thirteen signatures on fifteen pages."

"That's banking for you, lots of signatures. You know more about legalities than most," Cyn murmured. He knew Mykle was a past lawyer from Ardent Bailiffs, and he smiled at the thought of what they had to discuss. He paused and opened a drawer to reach out a document. "This is what bank lawyers have to deal with," Cyn said.

Mykle looked at the Confoundation law reference *Duty to Investors*. "Yes, yes." He sounded irritated. "I've seen all that. What does the other one say?" He flicked a dismissive backhand to shoo away the infotainment volume on the desk.

Cyn noted the gesture. "Ah, yes, I thought you'd want that version."

He went to his files again and took out a package of documents that he placed on the desk. "We have a better banking guide with fewer documents. We've got it down to five pages and we only need four signatures. All we, let's say... all you do is add this to your contract and you get people to sign two promissory notes for two loans to buy tax shelters." Cyn tempted Mykle. "For all the money you want."

"That's more like it, how do you do it?"

Cyn warmed to the plan. He put his hand on the guide and nudged it along the table, towards Mykle. He began to think it would work out. They all wanted the same thing. "Well that's the point; we don't... do it, that is. We have to set you up as a bank agent. It means you have to get people to sign waivers that bank agents are client's agents." He lifted his hands with outstretched fingers and raised his shoulders and bobbed his head with a shrug. "It's all this legal stuff we have to work with. We have to be sure your sales people fill out documents. You know, when you buy a car and a salesperson does an application for a loan in the showroom to finance it. It's all done right there. You sign for a loan, we approve it and you get the keys to the car you want."

He paused. "It's the same, except with structured investment vehicles, people don't drive and they still owe the bank." He smiled at the pun. "You have to sell these at seventy-five thousand loonies a unit. You lend twenty-five, we lend fifty." He looked at Mykle. "We've got to be careful about not being seen to be involved. It's important we're not held liable for endorsing investments, or anything to do with loans that sell them. Investment sales and loan applications to close sales have to be done separately, at least from a legal point of view."

He looked at them both to confirm they understood the situation.

"It means you have to promote property and find people who want to buy it, just as you would anyway. If investors need financing, you need a sales rep to get them to sign bank documents they send to us, right?" He continued: "We simply use information you send us about them and their finances to fill out loan applications and check if you pre-approve the right sort of people. You send signed notes to us to evidence loans. We confirm their credit, and you get their money."

"So we're third-parties to bankers?" Daveh asked. Mykle could have answered, but he thought better of it as a test, and nodded in approval of what he heard. Cyn passed it well enough with a quick reply.

"In these deals you can use sales reps as go-betweens. They have to do everything to sell a loan. But we can't do anything unless clients sign they're not agents for the bank. It will be better for you if the MOB isn't held liable." Cyn sounded a bit threatening as he stifled a laugh: "Harrumph, we take care of it in the paperwork. Okay?"

Cyn's innuendoes worried Daveh who missed the point and mangled her words: "What-chew talking about? What kind of paper?"

"Er, you have to use our legal document we write to cover the angles. It's important you know how signature affidavits work. They have to be done right." He swiveled his chair to lift a legal size document fastened in a large cardboard staple corner from his desk drawer.

Cyn folded a page over the corner and said, "It has to be legal. You can't change the script, but you can customize blanks for instructions. That way you can make a sales kit with all the forms we need in your materials to handle loans. There are only two references to the MOB in the top left corner that we staple through the name for obvious reasons. The intent of borrowing is covered in a statement of affairs that they sign and you send to a financial institution of your choice."

He emphasized the point: "That'll be us to fill out the note." He paused.

"The loan agreement includes two loans. We need clients to initial the personal loan option to confirm they want to finance their investment. It's amortized over twenty-five years with a ten year term to look like a mortgage." Cyn glanced at Mykle and thumbed his way to a cheque-sized note tucked inside the corner. "This is the demand note you have to get people to sign and leave blank to fill out a loan to close the sale."

He looked at it thoughtfully. "The bank's name is on it, but it's small type, and hidden, see?" He opened the cardboard corner and removed the staple to show how it covered the note except the red dot for a signature. "We have to separate it from the contract that we check is signed and dated and properly witnessed signature before we rubberstamp the bank's name on our note for a 'Sitting Duck' loan."

Cyn looked up with a strange and twisted smile as though he just realized what he'd said. He set the papers down and they looked at each other a bit slack-jawed. Cyn couldn't stop himself saying, "We help you target a 'Sitting Duck' with good net worth." He swallowed. "You wouldn't want us refusing your loan referrals, would you?"

No one spoke; Mykle or Daveh might have blurted a witticism about what they thought of Cyn talking about 'Sitting Duck' loans. Daveh was still thinking when Mykle answered Cyn's question with a grunt of appreciation for his candor and dark humor about banking.

Cyn looked pleased with himself as he continued to explain procedure. "Our forms are in the appendices." He pointed to several attachments. "This is the bank's 'Affidavit of Subscribing Witness' that has to be notarized by a Commissioner of Oaths... you know, when sales reps testify they witnessed investors signing financial documents."

He pressed an index finger on the all-important page. "We need signature affidavits to identify people that sign agreements for you to handle loans in their names. We do everything behind the scenes to adjudicate people's credit. We'll soon let you know if they don't have sufficient assets. You might call them, but I'd say there's no point if they don't know about bank loans. It's between you and them. Best leave it to find another sitting duck. There's lots out there."

Cyn noticed Mykle twitch a faint grimace from blunt conversation and he said, "Don't worry; I doubt you'll get any like that, it hardly ever happens. After all, it's up to your reps to find good prospects."

Daveh spoke: "How's that?"

"We're only concerned about capital and interest. We want you and your sales people to pre-approve clients from a profile that targets high income and net worth." Cyn found a page he lifted and turned to show them both sides. "This is a tax-worthy statement of affairs," he said. "When you make a sales pitch for people to buy property from tax credit savings, you qualify them by how much income they earn. You have to ask for personal and financial information and they have to sign it, see?" He pointed to a red dot signature line. "You use the document to assess people's tax credit savings." He returned the form in its place in the package. "We use it to fill out loan applications."

"The information you need to assess people being tax credit worthy is the same as creditworthy. You sell investments, we sell loans."

"The form is the same as personal loan applications except there's no reference to the MOB. We fill out loans from what you send us on these and we call you if we need more information." He shook it in the air and put it back in sequence in the contract. "The main thing we need is an affidavit of subscribing witness so people don't have to sign bank loans or anything. We don't have much trouble if your reps do a good job screening. Anyway, if they come back with poor credit, I'm authorized to override alerts for more than we need…" he corrected himself… "er, you need from MOB loans to close sales."

"Do you call them?" Mykle valued Daveh's question about investors as another test to see how far Cyn would go with deception.

"Usually we don't call applicants. We might an easy mark. It's best if they don't hear from us. According to regulations we're supposed to call to confirm terms and conditions, but we assume your sales reps explain all that. You know the same as car salespeople tell buyers when they fax loan applications before they close sales and hand out keys to drive away. You get the money and we confirm terms and conditions when we write them to request monthly payments."

Daveh spoke up: "But in your example, customers fill out everything when they sign loans in showrooms to buy cars. Borrowing to invest is a totally different business." She glared at Mykle in exasperation. "Look, if our sales reps say no cash down, it's going to be a pretty hard sell if we turn round and ask people to fill out loan applications to borrow a bundle to buy property."

Mykle raised a hand. "We have to see if they have income to qualify, so we don't have to tell them. There's nothing wrong saying no cash down, it's true. We tell them about operating costs and the mortgage. It's a way of converting an investment liability into cash." He leveled his hand. "The bank has to tell them about their loans if they qualify."

"Well if you say so, but how do we get people to fill out forms without them catching on they're signing applications for bank loans?" Daveh wondered as she raised an eyebrow to question Mykle.

"Like I said, we don't tell them. They don't have to fill out the forms. All we want is sales reps that are good at getting people to sign 'em."

Daveh looked at the PLSA – Personal Loan Service Application – on Cyn's desk. "I've seen one of these before. When I applied for a mortgage, I opted for income loss insurance. It's on the form, what if someone wants insurance?" she said, pointing to the document.

The men glanced at each other in amusement if not exasperation; it was Cyn's turn to add clarification: "This isn't the form that goes in the sales kit. We only need a tax 'Statement of Affairs'. Look, if you talk about insurance you'd have to talk about debt,

54

which we don't want people to think about. We don't mention insurance, and no one ever asks." He left it said, and the conversation abated for a moment.

Cyn gestured to the papers. "People never read this stuff anyway, and after they've signed it, they don't see it again. It's only paperwork. We can work with blank pages or any old guff you send us. We use computers and with today's systems we can find out about people to fill out equity loans. Still, it's better for us if we know the client."

"Maybe the bank should do the selling. You can tell us how rich people are." Daveh was just a bit too quick in her mind to hold back. The sound of sarcasm came through in her voice.

Cyn ignored the jibe. "We have a hit list we can give you." He displayed a list of names on a screen and pressed Print, then in a condescending tone, "Look I've told you, all we do is sell loans. That's our business. You sell investments, right?" Daveh nodded. "Right, well we can't be seen to have a vested interest even though loans are used to claim credits. You have to announce it in the market and get financial advisors to do the selling, not us."

He sounded done, and sat back to compose himself. He murmured, "Explaining what these loans are about is not good for sales. We need debt. You don't want people asking questions before they sign."

Cyn took a breath. "We look on your business as a 'Point of Sale' for loans. You need to create a sales force we can work with. People who walk the talk. People who know how to close business. People who have clients' confidences, like accountants who know what we want."

Daveh followed and said, "Accounting firms send people to our product announcements." She raised an eyebrow. "I guess it's okay, but how will they know what to do?"

Cyn didn't hesitate. "If they do income tax returns they can prepare people for tax shelters. These things sell on not paying tax, which is what people like to hear. Accountants are good at it. They even fudge numbers so people think they need tax benefits. It's an easy sell, and it's common practice for accounting firms to work with brokers for commissions. All they have to do is follow the bank script."

It was Cyn's segue: "We have a seven-step process for what we call 'Off-site Loans Closings'. It authorizes you to run a BWAB." He glanced at Mykle to explain: "Bank-within-a-bank. This is from head office," he said as he gave each of them a copy. "It allows you to pre-approve bank loans. You need to know how it works, which bank documents you have to fill out, and what you have to send us."

Cyn wanted to make it clear: "As a BWAB you have everything you need up to step five. You have to integrate bank steps with your own procedures. Then we take over." Cyn read the transaction: "*Step one; obtain all the relevant information on applicant* (that's the client) *from promoter* (that's you) *and properly research the application immediately upon receipt* (that's us)." He eyed Mykle. "The project part is done already. All you do is check what you send is properly signed and dated." He continued: "*Step two; once all the stipulations of authorization have been met closing documents are to be prepared for promoter, highlighting areas where signatures are required.*" Cyn advised, "We give you forms with red dots on them ready for the job."

Cyn picked up his sales package and handed it to Daveh. "Selling starts here," he said with meaning. "Step three says you get contracts signed ASAP so we can get on with loan referrals." He glanced at the forms and looked up and smiled as he continued, "*Step four, the promoter* (that's you Mykle) *is to complete Affidavit of Subscribing Witness for each loan application (Appendix 4).*"

He looked at Mykle intensely. "We talked about this, right? When your sales reps go to a Commissioner of Oaths to witness signatures. As a lawyer you have to notarize them yourself and send them to us with the investor note, our note and loan application in one package."

Cyn grinned. "Do you have a bill?" He held his hand out while Mykle eased a clip wallet to unfold a banknote. Cyn took it and tore it in half. He kept one side and gave half back to Mykle. He spoke as he stapled his half to the package. "You send us half a deal. Your half is worthless until we approve your client's credit for a loan. Their cash 'papers' your note, it closes the sale for you to make money."

He continued reading: "*Step five, upon receipt of documentation from the promoter, complete audit of all documentation prior to releasing funds. We suggest that audit and processing be centralized at an Area Office to ensure effective control.*" He put the document in his in-tray and said, "We do it here, the Osowega branch. We approve as many as we can for as much as we can." He nodded to indicate job done.

Cyn patted the papers. "*Step six, subsequent to approval and prior to advancing funds, the customer is to be contacted by a Bank Officer, to review all terms and conditions of authorization.*" At this point he lifted himself up and sat on his hands. He pursed his lips in a silent whistle, and rolled his head about a couple of times. Then he eased his hands free and turning to his computer he brought his right forefinger down on the Enter key with gusto, like a flamboyant pianist energizing a singular high note. He then lifted the torn bill and gave Mykle's half back as he had said he would. He handed him a roll of clear tape and tilted his head and squinted an exaggerated lopsided wink.

He smiled. "This is a non-bank note, ready to paper," he clucked.

"*Step seven, immediately after the funds are advanced a letter of confirmation (Appendix 5) is to be sent to each individual investor.*" He set the MOB's no-wrong-doing guidelines aside. "We wait a week and send it out with a letter requesting twelve postdated cheques."

Mykle stuck the tattered note together and symbolically pretended to sign it. He put it in his wallet. "How quickly do you approve loans?"

"We need a week or two, longer with credit issues. It depends on you. It'll be much quicker for everyone if you get all the red dots signed in sales calls. That's what we expect you to do." Cyn waited for them to nod to indicate agreement. "We give you loan applications with red dots where we need signatures. Good salespeople get deals signed in about fifteen minutes. No more than half an hour."

He glanced at Mykle slyly. "The only delay might be your sales reps getting to notaries to witness signatures. Hmm?"

Daveh interrupted to repeat the walkthrough, "So it's really a job for accountants who do tax management and people's tax returns. All we have to do is get signed forms to you, you send us the money, and we calculate the interest for clients to claim tax credits." She raised an eyebrow. "Do we send receipts to clients, or accountants?"

"That depends on the accountant relationship," Mykle said.

Daveh spoke slowly: "If we sell no cash down, and if they expect to make mortgage payments to own property and you only send them a letter requesting postdated cheques, and they only report a mortgage for tax deductions… but we have the mortgage." Daveh looked at Cyn and wondered out loud: "You fill out notes for personal loans, right?" She realized and turned to Mykle with a half-surprised questioning look. "How the heck do people know they applied for bank loans?"

Mykle was stroking his chin and he nodded his head. He would have spoken, but Cyn cut in: "Some of them don't ever figure it out, even when we collect years later. But by then any wrongdoing is well past statutes of limitations." Cyn let it sink in. "It's legal, there's nothing for us to worry about… it's all up to you… what you say to clients, we don't care as long as we make quota selling loans."

Mykle said, "I don't care either, if you want me to notarize signature affidavits to make notes to make sales I'll do it. I just want money."

"Ah, yes, that reminds me, there's a clause in the agreement where a client authorizes us to release loan account funds… er, to you. It's something else to customize, you have put a name where it goes in the script. I recommend you get an independent law firm to set up an interim account for us to credit debit new client accounts."

"Got it." Mykle saw the reason: "We'll do it through my old firm."

The printer stopped listing prospects and Cyn handed the pages to Mykle. "Do they notarize affidavits, Mykle?" he asked him cheekily.

"Yes! Ha ha… you've done your homework. Good idea."

"We're not the only ones doing these, there's lots out there that'll sign a name to anything," Cyn said casually. He picked up loan package pages and shuffled them together with a tamping motion on his desk. "Good, well that's pretty much all there is to it." He peeked over the papers he finished arranging. "We'll have to check the sales package before it goes out. Legal will want to go over it to make sure it's bulletproof, but other than that, we leave everything to you."

He sat back in his chair while they looked at each other as contented schemers. Mykle rubbed his hands together and Cyn continued: "I've put the eighty-nine into our system already, we use a prefix for people to cross-reference our loans to your product code. It's all set to go. We only have to wait for a friend in Head Office to approve it."

He turned to his computer and typed a message, this time he clicked the keys with purpose. "I sent a message to Central Region, I want to check where we are with your submission for funding." He looked, "Er, nothing yet, I'll call and find out."

He dialed and spoke about Kaleidoscope. "He's here now." He paused. "Yes, we discussed it... I'll tell him." He put the phone down with a smile. "Our friend approved it." He stretched his hand out to shake Mykle's, which automatically reached out for the moment. "Okay?"

"OK!" Mykle leaned forward and released a quick sweaty grip, He sat bolt upright and rubbed his hands on his knees to dry his palms on the trouser cloth. He sat stiffly, and pressing his hands into the fabric with his elbows turned out. He looked and felt happy as Cyn continued.

"The contract will be here tomorrow. Head Office will have the usual conditions for you to sign, it's just details; project amounts, units, client profile, dates, terms, etc. You will have to sign a MOB 'Off-site Loans Closings' agreement that allows you to handle loans and use bank documents, the way we just talked about. Okay?" he confirmed.

"Right, no problem. We could start soon?" It was a question.

"Shouldn't take more than a week, you can be rolling, probably mid-September. This is one project. I expect you'll want to talk to us about another, was it 'Hillti' something you mentioned for next year?"

"Ninety Hilltop Lace." Mykle sat back visibly relaxed, and then he spoke to Daveh: "We'll finish our promotional video for the eighty-nine." He looked at Cyn and turning his head a movement caught his eye and he said, "There's something flashing on your computer."

Cyn laughed. "Oh, that." He turned the screen round to show them: "'Set Your Sights on St Lucia', it's on all our lending screens."

"They're really pushing us to sell debt. This year's prize is St Lucia." He rhymed to the Conga, "♫♫ We're going to St Lucia, ♫♫ to spend our filthy lucre, ♫ duhmmm ♫ dhmm ♫ dhum♫..."

Daveh couldn't help herself: "♫ Mmm ♫♫ very nice, are you going?"

He looked at her, then at Mykle. "I have a few deals going; with this one... it should rate for sure."

"What if we borrowed on investors' notes?" Mykle thought out loud.

"We recommend it. I hoped you'd see it that way. It'll be a cinch." Cyn was gleeful. "This is our way of making money make sense."

Mykle quipped, "Makes sense to me, more than Cybecie."

"Humph, way better. Nothing goes wrong, MOB legal makes sure of it," Cyn said with a satisfied look. He made a fist to jab his thumb in the air over his shoulder, "I have to report 'Sitting Duck' loans to Phil Morrsacs as savings. It does wonders to his bottom line. Ha ha ha."

They all smiled at each other with the faintest of nods in complicity. Cyn looked at them and rested his hands slightly apart on the papers in front of him. He smiled as if he had nothing else to talk about. His new agents took the hint and Mykle and Daveh rose to leave. Cyn stepped round his desk to open the door and see them out.

"Oh, don't forget this," he said. Cyn turned and picked up the paperback he had offered when the meeting started. "It's nothing really, hehe," he laughed, but it sounded slightly forced, even nervous compared to more recent chuckles. "I think you'll like it, it does everything we talked about. Just the way you want..."

Mykle turned and took it in his left hand that moved up and down up and down in sympathy with his right hand in another spontaneous handshake. "Mmm, thanks."

He read the title out loud, "*The Perfect Sting*," and from its back as he turned it over, "Bank Loan Game rules for Sitting Ducks."

Daveh watched Mykle as he put the volume in his briefcase. They left the bank together for the car park without speaking. Mykle looked serious as he contemplated the law for what next. And Daveh looked thoughtful as she absorbed new meaning about bank credit and the prospect of her new career in finance with Kaleidoscope... getting people to promise to pay debt to make money.

They Do No Wrong

For the longest time, Robby's casual knowledge of accounting had been from the sidelines of serious disinterest. He remembered being told accountants never made mistakes, only 'credit/debits'. It's an inside joke, something you have to understand to see the funny side. Accounting is what it is. Robby had a poor attitude, with no interest or aptitude for a career in tabulation. He held it in such low esteem it would certainly take a more serious personality than his to do the job.

Robby had visions of a dour Dickensian character alone in a dingy room, working by candlelight to balance transactions to a quarter of a penny. The austere stereotypical character doesn't come with birth, but is acquired from years of number-crunching. Solemnity is a gift bestowed and becoming to those that join the profession.

He was sure he wanted nothing to do with it. But there was no escape from crazy numbers in a dreamlike *Alice in Wonderland* world. He was a victim and witness to what he thought was fraud, inevitably and irrevocably drawn into something beyond his comprehension.

Robby's attitude and stubborn ignorance made him a magnet for a clever con. It's fair to say he and many more are taken in from time to time. Easy cons go unnoticed. How would people know? Most live simple lives. They are sublimely unaware their credit could be stolen by someone with devilish guile to deceive.

There are so many traps and the rising tide of debt is proof positive accounting is an important matter of personal concern. As if life isn't complicated enough. But it is, and it worsens every day. The more there is in the news about bankers, advisors, accountants, lawyers and realtors, the less people trust them. Especially those that really enjoy the work.

Modern day complexities increase the odds for honest mistakes and errors in accounting, but ever more likely, deliberate and calculated fraud. Robby knows that now, but he still holds on to a faint hope that someday he'll get over being forced into the subject.

It's a myth that accounting is a numerical science, that credit debits fix all errors. It's quite exciting, really. More like financial miracles.

Money's Our Business

"You know exactly what it's about, and who it is, I am!"

The call started with a screech and ended with a loud crash of a phone slammed down in anger. Robby hadn't a clue what it was about, or who was on the phone. He figured something… he knew for sure it was a serious caller with a serious message.

It was all about money. The lady on the phone had told him so in no uncertain terms… stop playing games, and pay up lots. Right away!

It wasn't a good day to reach Robby. A thirteenth is time he tends to spend in quiet reflection. He hasn't yet figured if a thirteen is a good omen for him, or just plain bad. Whatever… when a thirteenth turns up, he sees foreboding in it, and looks forward to its quiet passing.

The call found him in the kitchen where he sometimes works near the coffee pot. Robby was in a soulful reverie when the phone rang on a Friday thirteenth in February at the start of a new century.

The voice gave him a jolt and he was slow to catch on. It was thick with anger, accented and quick. It immediately put him on edge. But to a large extent he was simply stunned and stupefied. All he could think was to ask what it was about. It got him nowhere.

"You should have settled this, a year back! And you know what it is that I am talking about!" it went on, sounding shrill, loud, and foreign. Robby remembered asking, several times, "Who are you?" But there was no answer to the question. All he knew was the lady said it was her job to get money from people like him.

His heart ached. "It would be a help if I knew what you were talking about. Please… just tell me who you are." But the phone went down in anger, leaving him quiet, in deep concern.

Robby was poorly seated on a high kitchen barstool at a raised table. It had become his place to work on a laptop computer from time to time. He used to have a separate office to himself in a previous life in a different house. Today he worked a timeshare with domestic chores.

His wife, Bobbie, said he had strayed too far from a room downstairs. It was a mass of boxes after moving and he hadn't found the heart, or the will, to sort through things yet. He might get to it, someday.

Actually, he hadn't organized work things for years. His office was like a disaster area where in the absence of a bulldozer everything remains a heap, like a child's room that never gets sorted because the occupant is completely unaware, incapable, or simply traumatized like Robby. It was as well the mess was out of sight round a corner in the basement. Still, Bobbie would have liked a door to hide the mess from anyone who might peek in that direction. Something to separate it from an otherwise perfectly clean and tidy sanctuary they called home.

The phone was on the kitchen wall, and Robby stared at it for a while. Bobbie was out to work and there was no one to talk to. Time drifted and presently he poured another coffee and sat down to think it over. Then it dawned on him. The phone was fitted with a new-fangled call display feature, and the caller's number might be saved on the handset. It was. All he had to do was press the dial button.

The business trained voice was easy to recognize and Robby started with his name and a question, "Was that you... just called me?"

"Yes!"

"OK, can you tell me who you are?"

There was jazz singing in the background as the lady identified her company and occupation: "This is the MOB and I'm in collections."

He knew he was paying down a mortgage with the bank.

"We have a loan in collections and it's my job to find you and make you pay it."

Robby was surprised. "But I am still making automatic payments, the MOB knows that, why is it in collections?"

"You know we want the money and I've been told to get it."

Robby had been in touch with the bank and he recalled a recent conversation with a branch representative. He asked the lady, "How can I have a mortgage at a branch and also in collections? And why are you chasing me while I'm paying it down?"

"We stopped your payments. You'd better call the Osowega branch."

"All right, but I want to tell you, this call is a surprise, it's very upsetting, and I don't have the health to..."

"I have it now. You'd better call your account manager." That was all she had to say. The phone went down with a loud click, dead... again.

In fact Robby was shaken. He couldn't bring himself to phone anyone right then. He had talked about the mortgage a while ago. The MOB had written him about it after paying it for some eleven years to own commercial real estate from an investment. His accountant had told him the mortgage would be paid out from an upcoming sale.

But the MOB wanted money now.

The previous year they asked for an update on Robby's circumstances to continue monthly payments or renegotiate the debt. The conversation resulted in a representative telling him he could continue his monthly payments. She had sounded pleasant, even sincere. "You people have had a rough ride on this," she said sympathetically.

"I'll be glad when it's sold," Robby agreed from the heart. "Er… thanks for renewing the mortgage."

Robby didn't realize why she said what she did, or what she meant by a rough ride, or how naïve he must have sounded, until years later.

That was how it stood just a month ago in a letter to confirm the MOB's competitive rate and new payment amounts. The branch had emailed the conversations, and Robby had replied with a covering letter with the details they wanted about his health and income.

It seemed to him he had done what they wanted, and as far as he knew he hadn't missed a payment, which was a stretch on family resources. It consumed his savings in a steady downward spiral.

It was like Robby had a hole in his pocket. They were approaching retirement and he was looking forward to his daughter's graduation. They hoped to manage on a smaller income in later years. It wasn't easy, but Robby thought things would improve when the investment property was sold for the mortgage to go away.

But this call was completely opposite to his understanding, and all he could do was phone the MOB to find out what was really going on. When he spoke with a representative she said it was out of her hands, and he would have to talk to the branch manager. "Mrs Church will speak to you now…"

The bank manager set the tone immediately. "We've already told you to pay this loan and you haven't done that."

"But I wrote you about it and I have a letter from you about making automatic payments."

"Not any more. We canceled all that. We're not accepting any more payments from you." Robby held the phone and remained quiet. "And don't call here again, I've sent your loan to collections. Goodbye."

The phone went dead.

Business Accounting

Robby enjoyed meetings over coffee and having business lunches from time to time. This was one of the meetings to see his friend Gofa, to catch up with news and pick up a document he thought was somewhat overdue.

They hadn't met for several months and Robby was looking forward to a good brew and a man-sized portion of fish and chips. He wasn't disappointed about the hops, the catch, or the conversation.

It was about two years since the bank called him about indebtedness, and a lot had happened in between. Robby's persistence had won him a judgment to counterclaim and challenge the MOB's claim against him. It was an unusual development. His new lawyer advised a case that his accountant and the investment promoter both had a hand in creating debt. They had figured enough and had sufficient evidence to argue that third parties were involved in the affair.

Kaleidoscope Equities didn't exist by that name any more. It seems Avaloan bought the investment company with L'Æmori free to repackage and resell the same tax-shelter properties as REITs – Real Estate Investment Trusts. Robby had a problem with that. He thought his property managed by Kaleidoscope had been sold to someone else instead of L'Æmori apparently involved in a non-arm's length deal.

Robby didn't know much about Kaleidoscope because his accounting firm Fudgit and Perysh was the only contact for information.

Al Fudgit kept the company books. He taught Bobbie how to record business for annual reports and wages for personal tax returns. Robby and Bobbie were far too trusting and busy to think about any control they might have given up. Even if doubt ever crossed their minds they wouldn't have known any better to do anything different.

In Robby's business it was his job to plan the work, and work the plan. Bobbie did the invoicing and journal entries that she gave to Al at the end of each year. Al would write the annual reports and arrange a time to discuss the numbers. His focus was to follow the rules. "The numbers have to work," he said, and Bobbie did a good job keeping careful records that followed Al's instructions to the letter.

So did Robby Ducky. He was an energetic man, and it was his good fortune to pioneer process redesign methodology to improve business analysis for more success-ful applications of computer technologies.

Robby had the ability to visualize systems from conversations about business, and vice versa. He was blessed with a dry sense of humor that was always on focus and made him a popular team player with clients. People said he was a good business analyst and he became known for his approach that involved people in a customer-focused setting to prototype business solutions before systems' development.

Robby had fifteen minutes of fame from writing workshop materials adapted for best IT project management practices. He found time to write on flights between jobs, and mostly late at night in his office. He was a bit of a workaholic and generally preoccupied with systems.

Accounting hardly ever crossed Robby's mind.

Going into business was good for Robby, and those around him.

Annual yearend meetings became a routine that generally showed his ignorance of accounting. It was a point of amusement to everyone. The company did well and he was only expected to ask or answer simple questions, nod wisely, sign papers, and get right back to work.

In Al's experience Robby wasn't good at signing papers. For one thing he was rarely in his office. And even though it was only steps from home there were several yearend reports left unsigned. It was just that financial papers generally found their way to the bottom of a heap in the office in-tray. Al asked Bobbie to chase papers, but it didn't help much, so he devised his own way to solve the problem.

Whenever Al wanted a signature, he would assemble pages and carefully position bright fluorescent Post-it arrowheads for signatures. He would lift pages for Robby and hover and point to places to sign with a free hand. Robby would ask if it was all right, and Al would say it was fine, concluding, "We can do the accounting now."

The feel-good factor created a tradition with an invitation for Al to join company staff and family at an annual Christmas party. It wasn't a big concern, but it took up a good-sized table in a restaurant.

As well as company records and annual statements, Al would talk to Robby about personal income tax. That was how Robby got into the Kaleidoscope mess; nothing worked the way Al said it would. Over time, the Duckys would ask about the rent from property that should have paid down the mortgage. Al mostly answered, "Don't worry, you are still better off with tax credits" or "Right now they're looking for new tenants and things will improve." And later, after several years, "They're looking for a buyer. It'll all work out when it's sold."

They were difficult conversations and Al complained to Bobbie that Robby was bugging him too much. Eventually they stopped talking about it. But when Al mentioned that Kaleidoscope was going to sell the property it got Robby to ask the question all over again, "When?"

And the answer came as always, "Soon, just wait."

But it wasn't soon enough. It was probably predictable that eventually Robby became ill to a point he could no longer do the work. In the end he saw so little of Al that he couldn't even remember to ask about Kaleidoscope.

It was a constant worry that turned into a nightmare when, after paying some two hundred thousand in so-called mortgage payments for ten years, the MOB finally wrote that Robby was mistaken. They said he didn't own property with a mortgage. They said while he saved his tax credits he owed a hundred thousand loonies to a promissory note.

Capital Letters

"Yes sir, please hold."

"Mykle L'Æmori."

"It's Geosh, I'm calling about your process guidelines."

"Yes Geosh, what can I do for you?" Mykle waved to his assistant Marion O'Bleary to come over as he held his hand to shield the telephone mouthpiece. "The eighty-nine package," he whispered.

"We have to be clear that bank-demand notes must be left blank. I'm sending you a fax. It should be there in a few minutes."

Marion found the file and put it on Mykle's desk as the fax machine started. She went to check the page as it nudged out a heading and lip-synced upside-down letters – "Be-Owe-Em" – to identify its source.

"It's printing now," Mykle said. "Have you changed it much?"

"No, just the section about investors signing blank demand-notes."

"Right, if you hold on a moment we can be on the same page," Mykle said watching the fax paper feed line by line. The machine stopped printing and Marion advanced the roll to a rip-off line.

"It's here," Mykle smiled as Marion handed it to him. "Yes, I have it now." He scanned the page and quickly recognized the change.

"Hmm…" He read the heading. "Line 4, loan documents." He read it in silence. Geosh knew what he was doing and waited patiently until Mykle said, "It reads fine, we can retype ours, no problem."

"Good, that's what I want to hear." Geosh was matter of fact as usual.

He continued: "You made reference to a bank twice without naming it, which is correct. What you call a 'Net Worth Statement' is what we call a 'Statement of Affairs'. It's all right, but you have to add what I've sent after the signature line to make it an application for a loan."

Mykle read the last part of the fax out loud.

I authorize Kaleidoscope to obtain credit from the financial institution of its choice.

I certify that all the information in this Application is true and complete and understand that it will be used by the financial institution to determine my creditworthiness. I agree that the financial institution of Kaleidoscope's choice may give to, receive from, and share and exchange with others, including credit bureau and persons with whom I have or may have financial dealings, credit and other information about me.

"The MOB is our bank of choice and you want this after the signature ending the statement of net worth on page two," Mykle confirmed.

"Yes, but don't cite which bank." Geosh didn't want to discuss non-disclosure, adding, "How are you doing recruiting agents?"

Mykle noticed the duality and corrected Geosh – "Sales reps" – before saying, "Fine, we're on track, how about your loan packages?"

"We've had them proofed, we're set to print two hundred next week. They're embossed with red dots next to signature lines. We need to attach your contract pages with ours because they use a machine that staples all the pages together in a cardboard document corner."

"Good, we'll be okay then." Mykle was learning MOB culture and how to deal with Geosh. "We have a dry run with Cyn and Bræn on Monday, I'll have the changes done by then. Anything else?" he said.

"No, that's all. I'll call if there's anything, thank you Mykle."

"My pleasure." Mykle leered but not at Marion as he put the handset down. "Uppercase! He wants to make sure we capitalize his notes."

Marion and Mykle saw the funny side of what he said, and they both grinned with joy from an unintended pun.

"You're getting good at banking," Marion said as she looked at the fax. "I'll type out his DO NOT DATE THE DEMAND NOTES in capital letters, and the rest in small print," she said with a smile.

"It's their game." Mykle shrugged. "They make the rules," he said.

KALEIDOSCOPE LIMITED PARTNERSHIP 89

HOW TO SUBSCRIBE

Please complete the following documents:

1. SUBSCRIPTION AGREEMENT

    (a) sign, witness and date page 5 and complete information

2. INVESTOR NOTE

    (a) sign, witness and date page 4

3. STATEMENT OF NET WORTH
(for investors who are applying for 100% equity financing)

(a) complete all details listed on the Statement of Net Worth, sign and witness
(b) you will be required to provide 2 years proof of income which should include the front page of the last 2 years Income Tax Returns including a copy of the Schedule 4 and Schedule 7 for each year if applicable. (If self employed the bank has requested 2 years financial statements for the business)

4. LOAN DOCUMENTS

(a) sign and witness the loan documents included in the package as indicated (**DO NOT DATE THE DEMAND NOTE** as this document **MUST** be dated on the day the funds are advanced by the bank)

5. RETURN OF DOCUMENTS

(a) Return the completed documents to our office:

        Kaleidoscope Equities Corporation
        c/o Marion Bleary
        P.O. Box 13 Queen's Key West
        Ogstowne Hontaria M5J 1A7

If you require any assistance, please contact our office at 6360 0212.

Affidavit Scripts

"This should interest you, Al." He picked up a glossy brochure.

Al scanned the magenta cover that showed a jaunty black-and-gold-trimmed tricorn and a photograph of an elegant building with the words 'Exceptional Investment Opportunity' above a company name in bold gold letters, 'Kaleidoscope Equities Corporation'.

Al was at his desk, with Yul opposite speaking enthusiastically: "It came in yesterday's mail. They're giving presentations and recruiting sales reps next week."

Fudgit and Perysh worked in an accounting firm with a number of wealthy clients in Okivil near Ogstowne. Al was interested in selling securities and mutual funds to develop the old firm into more profitable business. Better than grunt work accounting they had to do for hourly wages. Al had more profitable things in mind.

"People moonlight securities," his workmate alter ego said. "Call them to register and we'll talk about how to sell them later."

Kaleidoscope offered a place to Al in the following Friday session. They sent an agenda and directions to get to the orientation. "There'll be coffee and sandwiches and a parking pass for an area near the main entrance. Do you have any questions? Okay, we'll see you then."

Al had the look of an accountant, or maybe a teacher. He was thirty-something with a dark buzz-cut graying round the temples. He was a bit shorter than average height with a slight build.

It was his work and by choice he wore thick-rimmed glasses. They made his bushy eyebrows look joined together over a chiseled nose. His face was narrow with a square jawline. His forehead was deeply grooved in cross-pattern horizontal and vertical lines. A beautician would probably recommend lighter frames rather than his choice that accentuated the furrows in his forehead. Two vertical lines deeply etched above the bridge of his nose made it look longer, starting above his eyebrows. It gave him a rather serious countenance that would quickly fade with the flash of a toothy grin under a dark bushy mustache. It seemed to exaggerate a wide and friendly smile.

Al enjoyed driving into the city. He had good reason, his friend and client owned a car dealership, and the arrangement allowed Al the first option on cars that came up with short leases to run. He could choose a car to match his mood, which was mostly fast and luxurious. This time he drove a roadster that was more than he could afford to own, but for a while at least he could enjoy it as though he did.

He took the shoreline into the city with the soft-top down. It was a scenic route. Traffic didn't give way for speeding but Al's car had acceleration that could overtake many that didn't. He sat comfortably in fine leather upholstery and burned rubber in the warm sunshine. He listened to music from headrest speakers and relaxed his grip on the dimpled tan leather steering wheel. As usual, the accountant in him mused about what it would take to own such an expensive car.

Al slowed down as he approached the Budsmoor Building on Façade. While waiting for traffic lights he pressed a switch for the top to lift out of a covered space and settle in position overhead. Magic. Pure magic. Al was pleased and he sensed looks of admiration for the performance. He locked the roof down with latches as the lights turned green to go through a gate with a sharp right turn into the parking lot.

He loved fine cars.

A grin was firmly cemented on his face as he walked in and asked a good-looking receptionist for directions to the Kaleidoscope meeting.

He was early and had time to seek out food and beverages. Al chose a couple of sandwiches and poured himself a coffee. He paused to pick up a chocolate chip cookie, and then returned to a seat at a table near the door where he'd left his briefcase.

He was nibbling food as people turned up. They did pretty much the same as he had done. The clock on the wall moved ten minutes past the scheduled time before a lady walked in and strode to the podium. She tapped the microphone making hollow annoying clicks.

It got people's attention with muted groans and grimaces.

Everyone looked in her direction as she coughed and smiled and said, "We have a few more people coming, we'll start in a few minutes."

Someone else arrived and looked relieved to see the meeting hadn't started already. He went over for a coffee and took an empty seat at a table to himself. It wasn't exactly crowded and the newcomer was quite content to sit alone.

In a few minutes, the lady returned with a dapper man and they faced the group. She went to the microphone and spoke a greeting to get people's attention. "My name is Daveh Gumn, and I'll have more to say about this wonderful old building, our office, and the outstanding investment opportunity it represents for you and your clients."

Daveh held the podium and leaned forward. "But first I would like to introduce our President, Mykle L'Æmori, who will start the meeting."

Mykle stepped forward rubbing his hands together as he looked at his audience. "I want to welcome you to Kaleidoscope Properties, and hope you'll enjoy our presentation and hospitality as we discuss the building." He broke his hands apart and raised his right arm in the air. He turned and waved it towards a framed picture of Budsmoor on a nearby artist's easel. He looked around and said, "This is a perfect investment for your clients, and even for yourselves. This is the last of our presentations and we've had an excellent turnout and show of interest in this great opportunity. We have people from accounting firms who will represent us to their clients and I thought you would like to get to know each other... before we get down to business. "Would you," he gestured for a woman at the front to start, "tell us who you are, the firm you represent, and what brought you here."

Attendees said something about themselves and it came round to Al's turn. He hadn't really paid much attention to anyone, and he didn't really want to get to know people. He said, "Hi, I'm Al with Fudgit and Perysh Accounting. We just heard about this, and if I was to say why I'm here, it would be because I love cars."

It got a laugh, the first of the meeting. He meant he'd enjoyed the drive, but Mykle took double meaning from what he said and he eyed him as a fish to reel in.

Mykle weighed up each attendee and made mental notes from first impressions.

With the introductions over, Mykle went into a sales pitch he'd done many times before. He described the building: "It's in prime location in the downtown core, and it's close to fine dining and interesting stores and coffee shops. The Budsmoor Building is steeped in history, and you'll notice we are close to the Saint Florence Market, which is an added attraction for our tenants."

"We have arranged financing with the MOB," Mykle said. "The best thing about the deal is no cash down, and no carrying costs."

Mykle showed a list of tenants and the rental incomes and expenses. "We have a private Offering Memorandum if required. What we have is an excellent sales package, which will help you coax clients into a buying mood. It includes: a video, brochures and charts, and spreadsheet accounting with income projections. We pre-approve clients for financing with a loan for investors that qualify for income tax credits. When you close a sale there are excellent commissions and bonuses." He looked around, but his eyes seemed focused on Al.

"Well that's a brief introduction, and we'd like to show you a video that explains some of the details. It's about thirteen minutes," he said. He pressed a button that started a video on a television screen.

The screen filled with magenta and a gold outline of a navy officer's tricorn. It slowly dissolved into an image of a boardroom with Mykle walking into the picture and his name captioned next to his title. It was the exact same room they were in. Everything looked the same, even to his clothes and appearance standing next to an artist's easel with the same picture of the Budsmoor Building resting on it.

Al noticed Mykle's habit of wringing his hands together when talking about money. He also did it on camera. He smiled to himself about the observation as he watched the performance. He started taking notes. But there wasn't much to write about, it was mostly geared as a real estate sales pitch for potential buyers. He wanted to know about sales.

Mykle spoke about the property with enthusiasm, and it sounded good. There was a difference to what he had said in person, there was no mention of a bank or any money required to become a shareholder. The video highlighted the key benefit of a government endorsed plan with 'No Cash Down' and 'No Carrying Costs' in large bold letters.

Mykle introduced Daveh in the video as she stepped into view with her name and title on the screen. Her talk was about the value of the property, the financing and rental incomes. The screen melted into a list of benefits with 'No Cash Down' at the top. Another line appeared with a voice-over, 'No Carrying Costs'. Daveh tended to drone as a line chart traced increasing profits above level operating costs over a picture of the property with a disclaimer she read, "Assuming typical tax deductions from the debt carrying costs." Finally the video listed the benefits before fading out with upbeat music and a photo mosaic of the Budsmoor Building as a distinctive landmark in city views.

When the video ended, Daveh stepped up and turned the tape unit and television off. She looked up and said, "At this stage we invite you to look around, read our brochures and enjoy a coffee while we break for a few minutes. We will join you in about five minutes to meet you individually and talk about Kaleidoscope operations and support and how you get paid from sales."

People stood up and a few of them milled around the coffee table. Some picked up brochures and company materials. Others looked around as though they needed to check they were free to leave.

The meeting that started with thirteen was down to six by the time Mykle and Daveh came back. They didn't seem to mind. Al watched them from where he stood. They walked about and met people to chat with for a couple of minutes. Two shook Mykle's hand and left. Then Mykle walked over to where Al stood waiting for a word.

"That was a pretty good line about cars," Mykle said.

"Well it was the only thing I could think of when you asked what brought me here," Al grinned. "Other than money."

"Ah, yes." Mykle smiled. "What did you think of the presentation?"

"Great," he lied, "and it's a really nice building."

"Oh, yes, we're very happy with it. It's going to be a winner."

"Do you have any other properties?" Al wanted to size the company and know more about what they were selling.

"We have several projects subject to financing. We plan to add two properties a year over the next several years."

"You seem to have lost people from the meeting," Al said, looking round.

"Some of them just came in for the brochures for their offices. They will probably call back. This kind of deal isn't for everyone."

"What kind of deal's that?"

"Property, people are still a bit nervous after all the fuss about the banks and all those apartments up for sale a couple years back."

"Did that affect your business?" Al sounded surprised.

"A bit, financing is still the issue; we have to work with mortgage guidelines from the government." He looked at Al critically. "You'll need to know how this works if you want to be in on it."

Al was interested and it showed. He nodded in agreement. "The government tightened the rules after bankers went to jail over mortgages to do with property flips," he said knowingly.

"We called it the 'Caddysheik' deal," Mykle said. "Trust Companies issued mortgages on future value. The sale would've gone through if the media hadn't got a hold of it, and do-good politicians hadn't poked their noses into the rent issue."

"I remember. It was in the news for months."

"We've changed a few things since then."

Al looked interested. "Like what?"

Mykle explained, "Well the 'Caddysheik' deal involved an affidavit to fake a hundred million loonie deposit from an offshore bank to finance the sale, then lots of affidavits to report sub-mortgages to the Land Registry to comply with the seventy-five percent equity rule."

He paused to face Al. "Our deals work the other way round."

"How's that?" He sounded keen.

"Well, we inflate property values to fund them, but we don't have to worry about the seventy-five percent mortgage rule. Investors that sign notes owe us money for tax credits. The capital comes from a bank that underwrites another note against investors' personal credit and net worth. That way all the debt is secured to people's wealth, instead of property value. We keep that on the books for ourselves. We accrue interest on investors' notes that we report as the mortgage. It means there's no need to report anything to the Land Registry or even to Revenue." Mykle shrugged. "So we're free to do what we want."

Al was impressed. "Phew, that's so gu-ood. And, with equity in the property offset like that, you could borrow on it again, anytime."

Now it was Mykle's turn to be impressed, "You're quick," he said.

Al was still thinking outloud. "And no affidavits to mess with either."

"Not for us. The bank needs signature affidavits for their loans, but that has nothing to do with land registration. The bank does all the paperwork and they keep the authorities out of our hair. Everything's done behind the scenes. All we do is report loan interest charges for people to claim the mortgage as an expense for a tax write-off."

Al thought he understood it. The prospect of fooling the government excited him. "It's pretty slick," he said. "Was it your idea?"

"Nar, not really, the bank we're working with was a big player in Caddysheik. When they tightened the rules they figured another loophole and made a few amendments to the contracts they'd used before. It gets better all the time. They do it for lots of investments. All we have to do is find clients to do with accounting."

Al recognized underhandedness in the approach. "Is it safe?" he said.

"Sure it's safe. The law says investors take the risk. We cycle a few payments to lock them in debt. When we stop distributions they still have to make payments to the bank. That's all there is to it. And, it's legal. You could sell so many of these and make so much money you'll need an accountant yourself." They laughed at the thought.

"Cory and I have been thinking about it. Accounting is in the family, and she's working on a license to become a limited market dealer."

"Well that's different, we're not looking for sales representatives... we want accountants to close deals." Mykle gave Al a quizzical look.

Al didn't miss the point and quickly confirmed, "That's OK, I'll be her agent as well as yours. No sales calls... she'll like that."

"Right, I guess you'll continue doing accounting jobs for the firm you work for, but I don't expect they'd want to handle commissions from you selling investments to their customers, eh?" Mykle queried.

"They won't if it's my company in her name." He grinned, "That's what we were thinking, maybe call it *Mecory Investments*."

"Well if you want to do business with us, you should register the company pretty quick, she's bound to pass the exam and you'll need to put the money somewhere. Watch you don't spend it all on cars."

They looked at each other. Al flashed a toothy grin and he laughed. "We've been thinking about that too. A sports car with a personal company nameplate... wouldn't that be great! Really great!"

Mykle put a friendly arm over Al's shoulder and said, "Come into the office. The bank pays commissions on loans that close sales. I'll explain what you have to do for the MOB."

Forensic Accounting

Robby met Gofa Beers' CFP (Certified Fortune Picker) through his association with people in the Kaleidoscope deal. Gofa was trained in sleazy tax shelter schemes by researching players in them. He wrote partners in Kaleidoscope tax shelters with an offer to do a forensic audit that was taken up by more than two hundred people.

Robby met Gofa at a meeting about the same time he heard from the MOB. It was Gofa's job to examine the investment, trace the money and report his findings. The review was in a busy hotel conference center that was packed full with about three hundred and fifty unhappy investors in attendance.

Robby arrived late and walked quietly along the back row. He found a seat and sat next to a lady who smiled and whispered a greeting. She said she was a lawyer for an Ogstowne government department.

Many people had heard from the MOB, and several had grudgingly paid bank-demand notes already. They realized things weren't right and wanted to know if there was any way to get their money back. They were all upset about the Kaleidoscope experience, and Mykle L'Æmori as the managing partner.

Gofa used an overhead projector to explain: the real estate, the debt position, the current cash flows, what people had, and especially what they didn't have. He was clear there'd been some mischief and was fairly upbeat about the possibility for legal recourse.

The way Gofa talked about the ownership of property wasn't easy to understand and there were issues as to how it was financed. He said partners could vote on selling the property to pay out the bank.

Gofa went on to describe loonies from bank loans to investors even though they weren't supposed to have paid anything up front. That's what people expected from the sales pitch, which described income from real estate after paying a mortgage. But Gofa's record showed about five million cash from partners in debt to the MOB.

The way Gofa talked about the deal, it sounded fraudulent.

Robby was bewildered about the massive injection of cash into the hands of the general partner. He couldn't figure how it could be, or where it had come from. He still thought in terms of a pre-approved mortgage. Al described it that way years ago, and more recently when he said it would be paid out from the proceeds of an upcoming sale. As far as Robby knew, he had always reported it as a mortgage.

Gofa's explanation sounded the same, but more complicated, he said there had to be enough from the sale for people to receive money after everything else was paid out. The numbers were in Gofa's report.

"There's nothing left," he pointed to detailed expenses, "due to an additional mortgage on the property."

Someone stood up, "Isn't our money secure with a mortgage lien?"

It was a question on everyone's mind.

"Well, yes and no, your money's shown here, but it's not a mortgage. Some of you wouldn't know, but... er... this is the money you, er, borrowed from a bank. It's what you paid to get into Kaleidoscope. The sales pitch told you 'no cash down', that it wouldn't cost anything to become a partner, but when you signed the contract you also signed up for a personal loan with a bank."

Gofa paused. "The money from the bank, your debt, gave them about ten million cash to sell a property with an existing mortgage on it for about five million. The new money from the bank was free title so... one offset the other, in terms of debt. It could, and should, have been used to pay out the first mortgage then it would have been more profitable for you. Instead, Kaleidoscope took out another mortgage for another five million... in the partnership."

His hand hovered over the displayed figures. "Now you, er..." He coughed and corrected himself, "Kaleidoscope... had cash from the ten million you just borrowed, that you have to pay back to the bank yourselves, plus five million in original debt, plus a new mortgage for five million, which is all free money to them. In other words, when you all signed up, they were able to triple the debt load, with all of you as first creditors, with rent that could barely support two mortgages. Let alone pay back what you owe the bank."

Gofa looked out at the attentive audience. "You all signed your credit to the promoter; you were set up with way more debt than you were told. In effect you gave Kaleidoscope ten million loonies to play with."

He paused again. "Your investment is supposed to be covered by the cash flow from rent. But doubling the mortgage liability didn't leave anywhere near enough to do that, so everyone's saddled with monthly payments. Still, the deal's written up as a tax shelter and the money is on record as individual personal expenses. It's an investment, so all the interest you paid qualified as personal losses for tax benefits. But you still owe the underwriting bank."

He looked around the room. "That's the long answer. That's why you have unsecured personal loans. That's why it's not a mortgage and it's why there's no registered lien to protect you as investors."

Then to emphasize the point: "If you'd seen a prospectus, you might have known. What we're talking about is unsecured personal loans to buy into Kaleidoscope against promissory notes for bank loans; if you haven't paid them already, the MOB will be calling you soon."

The room that had been quiet turned to a deathly hollow sound of silence. Then Gofa continued his talk: "You might wonder where all the money went… well that's a good question. The records show it seems to have gone into renovations and management fees."

He raised a brochure and said, "But about the same time it looks like Kaleidoscope bought another property and rolled it into a portfolio with the same financing scheme with the MOB for another deal. In fact Kaleidoscope and the MOB did several deals with L'Æmori as the managing partner with a majority vote for everything to be rolled up into group of properties, that some of you are still in today."

Robby couldn't recall being told there was any profit from the venture in ten years. The lesson was heavy going and too much to absorb.

Even though he knew how much was at stake his attention was dulled by the subject matter. In fact he was a little bored. He turned his head towards his conference neighbor, the lawyer for the city.

All Robby could say was, "The whole thing looks like a scam to me."

Robby's comment didn't get a response as the presentation continued; Gofa was saying, "Let's look what it means if you sell. Here's the debt in the existing first mortgage for five million and then another five million taken out in a second mortgage. And today, there's still about five million scheduled in management fees and renovation expenses. These are the operating expenses. There are fewer tenants paying rent. It adds up to about ten million loonies, which is more than income. It's not a good business proposition to attract a buyer."

"And I'm sure you understand empty space doesn't show well for a sale." He raised his voice. "The value in today's market is about nine million, maybe ten if it were better managed and fully occupied." He dabbed a pudgy finger on the loonies in the bottom line. "There's not much of a business case." The microphone amplified his conclusion he spoke in a hushed voice: "You'll be lucky to break even."

Gofa turned to a new chart that showed a list of possible actions. One of these was to fire L'Æmori as the general partner and find a new manager to build it up and sell it for the best price, then follow up with a class action lawsuit.

That was Robby's choice, suing Kaleidoscope, and he looked for any signs of agreement from the lady lawyer next to him. Several people talked among themselves and Gofa allowed time for investors to ask questions. Some people gave their opinions about the choices on the screen, but most of the questions were about money issues.

Gofa reviewed the pros and cons of a class action. But when it came to posturing, the general feeling among people was to be simply rid of the investment and put it behind them as a bad deal. Most opted for market valuation and the agenda closed with a plan for Gofa to get back to them with more information to discuss at the next meeting.

Sitting next to a lawyer, Robby's conversation covered the possibility of joining a class action. Mainly the difficulties, but they didn't spend much time on it. Instead the conversation got round to Robby's case. She said she couldn't act for him, but suggested a third-party defense using a lawyer who knew more about banking and investment deals.

Everyone left and Robby's crazy life with lawyers started in earnest.

Vested Interests

"So you see the problem?" Won J'Kobbs faced Gofa Beers.

Some two hundred investors wanted Gofa to make inquiries to find out what Kaleidoscope had done with their tax savings. He told them he would get to the bottom of things. Even get their money back.

It didn't happen that way. Money changed hands but none of it in restitution. Quite the opposite for people that paid Gofa to follow the loonies paid to lawyers to get it back. Lawyers and gofers kept what they knew to themselves. The so-called second mortgage that was a derivative was a secret for years to come, denied to the bitter end.

As requested the Land Registry found Façade on record in a deed of purchase concerning Mykle L'Æmori as expected if the money investors borrowed from the MOB paid for the acquisition. But the transfer of title showed that Kaleidoscope purchased Façade some two years ahead of it being sold in the market as a tax shelter. Now, much later in default, Gofa reviewed documents that in hindsight showed the mechanics of an extraordinarily convoluted scam.

Gofa felt chuffed about his findings. Along with the mortgage he had the smoking gun… a rent consignment for one loonie that guaranteed revenue to the mortgage holders. Investors would be pleased.

No wonder L'Æmori notarized paid witness of signatures for trick loans. He sold tied loans to sell his property. It was obvious investors had been misled. The MOB must have known there was a conflict of interest in an 'Off-site Loans Closings' agreement for Kaleidoscope defined as the agent for the bank and tenant in Façade selling its own head office paying rent into a mortgage sold as an investment.

The secret was out. Gofa broke down numbers to calculate the profit from a cozy relationship as clear as a bright Confoundation day. He filled out an ABCP 'Acquire-to-Distribute-and-Reacquire' Business Model to itemize cash flow of a mortgage derivative credit default swap with undisclosed encumbrances, and non-arm's length sales with undisclosed loans.

The analysis showed: 1) L'Æmori had a vested interest selling his own property; and 2) the MOB had a vested interest selling loans.

REIT [*] Property Acquisition ~ Tax Shelter Business Model

200 Investment *'Units'* at $75,000.00 each in *'Off-site Loans Closings'*

($5 M property with $5 M mortgage and $5 M Non-bank Notes plus $10 M Bank-demand Notes 10% simple interest model)

$5 Million Investment Property ~ Abusive Trust Scenario	
Bank *'Daylight Loan'* transactions:	
A. Bank loan dependent Non-bank Notes *'Papered'* at $25,000 each to close 200 *'Units'*	5,000,000
B. Bank-demand Notes behind *'Daylight Loans'* that underwrite 200 *'Units'* at $50,000 each	10,000,000
C. Closing includes $5,000,000 mortgage loan for Broker to purchase real estate *'for investors'*	5,000,000
P. Four times negative equity to investors subscribing to mortgage partnership in $5 million property	20,000,000

Investment Property Cash Flow ~ Tax Avoidance Doctrine	
Ten-year tax shelter loan interest:	
A. Broker collects $500,000 annual interest on Non-bank Notes for 10 years from investment	5,000,000
B. Bank collects $1,000,000 annual interest on Bank-demand Notes for 10 years from investors	10,000,000
C. Bank collects $500,000 annual interest on Mortgage for 10 years from investment	5,000,000
P. Subscription agreement interest collected from $5 million mortgage derived terms and conditions	20,000,000
Bank forecloses mortgage in default by Broker and consigns investment property to Broker:	
A. Bank assumes investors' debt to $5,000,000 Non-bank Notes as new *'Holder'* in foreclosure	5,000,000
B. Bank as DIP – Debtor in Possession sells property to Broker in non-arms length deal	(10,000,000)
C. Bank collects $5,000,000 outstanding balance of mortgage from Broker in default after 10 years	**5,000,000**
P. Investors' return on investment from $10,000,000 property consigned to Broker after 10 years	0

Tax credit savings loan accounts	
Government endorsed tax credits for thrifty people to save RRSP's ~ Registered Retirement Savings Plans:	
A. Investors claim same tax credits as Broker collects interest on Non-bank Notes for 10 years	(5,000,000)
B. Investors claim same tax credits as Banker collects interest on Bank-demand Notes for 10 years	(10,000,000)
C. (Mortgage is not in tax credit streams)	
P. Total profit to Banker and Broker siphoning cash from government tax revenues	(15,000,000)

Investment *'Off-balance-sheet'* and *'Off-bank'* profit and loss summary	
Interest collected for ten years:	
A. Broker collects $5 million interest on $5 million in Non-bank Notes through tax evasion [1]	**5,000,000**
B. Underwriting Bank collects $10 million interest on $10 million Bank-demand Note tax avoidance	**10,000,000**
C. Underwriting Bank collects $5 million interest on $5 million mortgage	**5,000,000**
P. Total Profit to Bankers and Brokers offset by investors' losses and government tax credits	20,000,000

Preplanned losses including property acquisition by foreclosure	
Bank repossesses property in mortgage foreclosure and pursues residual debt in Bank-demand Notes:	
A. Bank collects $5 million from investor's debt to Non-bank Notes in final disbursements	**5,000,000**
B. Bank collects $10 million from investors' Bank-demand Notes notarized by Broker Agent [2]	**10,000,000**
C. Broker acquires debt free property launched in market as new REIT - Real Estate Investment Trust	
P. Total amount in Promissory Notes **not** receipted as paid for investors to claim real capital losses [3]	(15,000,000)

Broker acquires $10 million property in foreclosure and Bank profits from agency relationship [4]	35,000,000

[1] *Investors use interest charges paid from real estate cash flows reported as personal expenses to claim income tax credits*
[2] *Bank collects debt to Bank-demand Notes based on photocopied notes that debtors must pay without receipt*
[3] *Investors cannot claim real capital losses without original notes stamped as paid*
[4] *Courts rule Broker is not Bank's agent as investors sign contra proferentum waivers stating the Broker is their own agent*
[*] *REIT – Real Estate Investment Trust*

Gofa worked hard for duped investors. He compiled materials in three volumes to file a complaint with the Conjurer of Securities. He felt confident he could present a strong case and he expected to tell his clients there would be an investigation. He said as much to Robby.

Won examined the numbers. "They'll never investigate this," he said.

Gofa knew it. The Conjurer closed the matter on receipt with a letter advising insufficient evidence and that it was a civil matter. In later years Robby wrote several complaints and got the same response.

Gofa looked at Won and thought of investors claiming ten years' interest charges on bank-demand notes behind codependent non-bank notes for an SIV to generate loan charges for personal income tax credits. It looked like massive tax evasion to launder worthless paper.

"You pay rent into your mortgage for investors to claim tax credits as if they paid it from personal income?" Gofa said dumbfounded.

"Mmmm," Won murmured, "good, isn't it? But it's their loss you see, it would be their gain if we gave them rent, but Confoundation tax credits don't work that way." He grinned at the thought. "If we paid rent to investors they would have to report it as income that would mean more tax to pay to the government. It has to be our gain to be their loss. This way we report investors' debt to save tax. That's how it works." Won made it sound normal. "Everybody wins."

"You syndicate your own office property for people to buy as income-producing commercial real estate with tied loans," Gofa said matter-of-factly. "The rent pays your mortgage while government pays interest on it until you default." He looked at Won. "Then… you reacquire the property with investors' IOUs and the MOB collects principal on bank-demand notes you notarized to sell it to them in the first place."

"They know all about it."

"Who?"

"The Confoundation."

"They condone fraud?" Gofa said doubtfully.

"They approve all kinds of tax credits," said Won, dodging the question.

"That doesn't mean people understand a scheme like this. Investors for sure didn't know about you notarizing signatures for bank loans. And I bet they've no idea they make fake money for you to launder for cash when you report the interest you collect for tax credits, eh?"

"Mmmm." Won conceded the point made in Gofa's tabulation.

"Don't you think it's a bit confusing? Mixing non-bank notes for tax evasion with bank notes for tax avoidance." Gofa sounded peeved. "It looks like a Ponzi scheme to me, and I have to answer questions."

"It's supposed to be confusing," Won said smugly. "That's how they want it. Look, the way Confoundation sees it, banks do no wrong and they're not responsible. They say it's a personal problem."

"So the government knows?" Gofa countered.

"Well, they look the other way so it continues." Won insisted, "Look, it's legal. Several banks went to the Supreme Judiciary in the Accuser case. Upstain ruled 'Caveat Emptor', that some four hundred people didn't read what they signed. The Gallows Prosecutor says they are sophisticated investors and they know what they're doing."

"Not with Ponzi rubberstamped and papered notes they don't." Won's obtuseness annoyed Gofa. He became belligerent for his clients. "Not the way you package documents and conceal notes for bank loans."

The men looked at each other in silence. It gave Gofa time to add, "You handle blank notes for a bank that has the gall to get judges to rule that people don't read what they sign. How could they when they're filled out later?" Gofa thought of Ducky's case. "Robby didn't sign for two units, and Bobbie didn't sign for a tax shelter."

Won knew everyone had a price and he persisted. "The government has to side with banks. It's debt that has to keep growing. That's why Justice Upstain ruled borrowers in the Accuser Case had to prove the agency relationship between us and banks."

"Would the mortgage prove such a relationship?"

"What mortgage?" Won looked at Gofa and he smiled as though he had something else to say.

"Yours." Gofa pointed to the line in the spreadsheet. "The one that's in foreclosure, the one you hid from investors."

Won looked at the spreadsheet again. "You've done your homework."

Gofa stood firm. "When it's sold… does L'Æmori pay back the non-bank notes, or are they included in the price?"

Won said calmly, "I thought you meant yours."

"What?" Gofa was taken aback and sounded confused.

"Its only business. You must see it our way." Won brought it down to graft. It was then Gofa realized there was an offer on the table.

"You have a mortgage, mmm?" Won twitched more than winked.

At last Gofa played along. "Not sheltered like yours," he said.

The conversation stopped, waiting. Gofa flinched. "I have to get back to the investors. We have another meeting in a couple of weeks."

Won implied agreement. "This is just between us. I'll talk to Mykle, he'll talk to the MOB. You won't have to wait that long," he said.

A REIT Good Thing

About a month later Gofa ran another meeting for investors. This time he wasn't nearly as bullish about a class action against Kaleidoscope. "Firing the general manager will probably just make the existing mortgagor want to refinance," Gofa said in truth to his clients. "That would mean a new rate of interest and possibly a cash-call just to keep things solvent." The idea of shelling out money to another call didn't go over too well to a group of largely beaten people.

A lady stood up and the place went quiet as people looked at her and realized she was crying. "My husband died with all this going on," she said, "and the MOB holds me responsible for a loan. He's dead and I have to sell my home to repay debt we knew nothing about." Her quiet voice was poignant as she finished: "I have nowhere to go, and I don't know what to do." She remained standing, heartbroken.

The distraught woman glanced at Gofa but he looked away. He had nothing to say. No one could think of anything to say. They looked at him to continue. Kaleidoscope had made another buyout offer a few weeks ago, but it had been rejected as not enough. It was too hard to swallow. Gofa thought of his agenda. A lady next to the woman gently touched her arm, and she shrank back into her seat. Gofa went on to say people should make the most of selling, in light of a new offer.

Won J'Kobbs had attended previous meetings for Kaleidoscope but this time Gofa introduced him to speak to investors. "We have another offer," Won said. "It has nothing to do with Kaleidoscope and it's a million loonies more than the last. It's closer to market value. You'd do well to consider it." That's all he had to say.

Gofa stepped up and went through the numbers again, saying the offer made such a difference people should think about it, and vote for it.

The advice went into the minutes of the meeting and Kaleidoscope sent out a ballot for people to vote to sell, or not. Robby spoke to Al who said it was a good offer. Al said his mother was a partner, and that she would vote for it. He recommended Robby do the same, to see an end to the money pit. The Duckys thought it was fishy, but there was general agreement to it by almost everyone. So they signed "Yes" to letting it go.

Getting rid of the property was one thing, but it didn't remove the problem of the MOB collecting trick loans. As predicted, people only received a pittance from the proceeds of the sale. And it wasn't long before Gofa called Robby about people's reactions. Gofa was upset. He said he'd had an earful from almost everyone concerned.

A most unsettling call came from a seventy-year-old lady who spoke about her husband. He was already frail and the stress was just too much to bear. He suffered a heart attack reading the letter of accounts and measly disbursements from Kaleidoscope. He died soon after.

Robby called Gofa as well, but not to complain. He was more interested in the new owner. It appeared to have been flipped back to the welcoming arms of Mykle L'Æmori as general partner selling Façade to establish a REIT in a newly formed company called Avaloan.

Gofa talked about complaints that continued. He was worried people had the wrong impression that he'd had something to do with the outcome. After all, he had made a strong argument for people to sell.

Robby thought… just acquiring an office block at a bargain basement price might be suspicious, but he didn't say what he thought of Gofa. He simply told him the news that L'Æmori was the buyer.

He had no idea the paper he signed that made exaggerated if not fraudulent tax claims for someone else's benefit should have been returned to him to cancel the debt. That little quirk would only be told in the fullness of time.

Anything but Worry

Robby had pretty much come to terms with the situation and the prospect of losing more than anything he'd ever lost in his life before. He knew he didn't have the money to pay, so it was something of a distant, if not a moot, point. His biggest worry was finding a way to fight back. He was anxious about keeping his home, and the constant endless worry of it wasn't doing him any good.

One day he was listening to a talk show about worry and it caught his attention.

> *...feeling helpless can be more a cause of worry, than the problem itself. The cure is to understand the problem and to figure out best options for a solution. Even if a problem appears insurmountable, you'll feel a whole lot better... just doing something about it.*

Robby knew it had affected him. His daughter said as much as he worked in the kitchen. "Daddy doesn't look happy these days."

Her Mom looked wistful, and said it was about money, and followed, "It's a pretty serious problem, that's why he has a long face today."

It was years ago. Robby's daughter was a cute teenager; now in her twenties she had large brown eyes that tended to melt people, some swooning sooner than others. She had a knack of flashing a disarming smile, and saying the right thing spontaneously. "Never mind Daddy, just think of your smile when you kick some butt, aye Dad?"

Robby wasn't likely to forget those words. It sounded more like him from happier times and younger days. Indeed he looked forward to a possible future when it might yet be true.

The airwaves continued talking about 'A' type people with larger than life personalities who simply thrive on problems and hardly ever worry about anything. It didn't matter. Robby got the message and it confirmed his own feelings; he had to figure out 'How' the MOB had taken such a hold on him.

Lawyers had told him 'Why' it was legal for long enough.

Robby always had time for a radio. He had one on whenever he did anything around the house, and especially when he was busy typing. Talk shows interested him the most. They inspired him and his ears perked up to seamy politics and financial scandals.

There was no shortage. Another program started with examples of shady practices of all kinds that make talk shows not only possible, but numerous and international. A guest speaker described similar scandals, and made the point that banks only exist to make money and will do anything for profit, especially for million-loonie paychecks and humongous bonuses.

That was the essence of a talk show that featured a brief discussion on business ethics. The panel's points of view ranged from a "nothing's changed" perspective, to the more optimistic-sounding "businesses are more aware and paying more attention to the issue".

There wasn't much disagreement among the guests on these airwaves; another person talked about teaching ethics and guidelines for better business practices, institutionalized rules and stronger enforcement.

The radio host went on to ask what ordinary people could do.

Robby spoke to the radio: "Not much." It spoke back in agreement according to the "nothing's changed" speaker. "As long as corporate governance remains in the hands of business executives who make the rules, we will see more and probably ever more creative scandals…"

In this panel discussion whatever hopes the public might think they had, the panel didn't have much faith in regulatory bodies, which they described as paper tigers. "They have no teeth. What *is* the point of voluntary guidelines for banks in this day and age?"

Maybe the radio went too far, it sounded nervous: "Well that's all we have time for today, I'd like to thank our guests, and leave a question for our listeners. Do you think most businesses act ethically? Have you lost your faith in them because of the scandals we have seen? If you want to share your thoughts, call our vox-box at 225 2525 or drop us a line at CB Station A, Ogstowne, Hontaria."

Robby wrote the station the same as he wrote complaint agencies that ignored him just the same.

Somehow he had taken out a six-figure loan with double-digit interest. It wasn't something he would have done knowingly, nor on his own. Bobbie would never have agreed to it, if they'd known. But they didn't. Robby couldn't remember doing it, and in his heart he knew he would feel a whole lot better if he knew exactly how it happened.

Robby's road to knowledge started with phone calls to people about Kaleidoscope. It put him in touch with more people in debt to the MOB than he would have thought possible. He found people ready and eager to talk. They all had something to say about L'Æmori.

Robby wasn't the only casualty. Not just him.

A conversation took place about the time partners voted to sell, which resulted in final disbursements. The deal had just closed when Robby heard some sobering news.

"Oh yes, the property you're talking about belongs to Kaleidoscope. You know they've changed their name to Avaloan, anyway they have it on the market as a REIT. It's on the web with pictures and everything. You'll know it when you see it."

Robby saw it and called Gofa right away to give him the Internet address. Gofa looked through the material while they were on the phone. He took a minute and said, "Darn, this would have taken months to pull together. They must have had it planned all along."

Robby slept on the news and the next day he called Gofa to see if he could rescind his vote. "This isn't the right time for that," Gofa said. He didn't give much of a reason, but it seemed to close the option. Still, not one to back off, Robby tried another approach.

"OK, what about this being a case for a Conjurer's inquiry?

Gofa said, "That should work, investment promoters aren't allowed to buy properties if they're engaged as partners. It's a non-arm's-length deal that should have been disclosed to investors when they voted to sell their units. It should be enough to go after L'Æmori."

"OK, let's do it," Robby told him.

That was months ago, almost a year, and although Robby called him to see how it was going, it took much longer than expected. Not that Robby knew what was involved, or even what to expect in terms of how long the Conjurer would take. He was probably impatient, but as time passed he wondered if someone else might do a better job.

One day, about six months since his last call, Gofa phoned Robby about the complaint about Kaleidoscope. "It went to the Conjurer to review, but they sent it back for lack of evidence."

It was another disappointment, and a setback. As they talked about it, Robby figured he would like to see what Gofa had actually sent. He called and said he wanted to see the complaint next time they met.

"Sure let's do lunch. I'll bring the file and we can go over it when we meet," Gofa said without hesitation.

Debt Dilemma

Gofa met Robby near his office and they went on to a pub for lunch. The CFP was a big man with a background in engineering that had probably molded him as a down-to-earth sort. He had an accounting office and an operating interest in a technology company. His face was large and round and it would break into a smile whenever he relaxed or had a good answer for things. And, although he dressed for work in a shirt and tie, he would sometimes loosen it and leave his collar button undone for a more casual look in his large loose-fitting clothes.

He was chatty about a problem. "Computers!" He was exasperated. "I haven't had an email for days, now I've got hundreds."

Robby sympathized and asked if he'd had more luck getting away for a break. "No, we've been busy with the in-laws after a car accident. Mom was driving and Dad's just out of hospital," adding, "She's not allowed to drive any more so I have to take them everywhere."

Gofa paused and concluded, "It's come at a bad time for us."

The two of them had a great lunch and enjoyed another binge on greasy food and frothy beer. They talked about ideas for consumer protection in the banking sector. Robby went over his troubles with the MOB, and Gofa spoke about his experience with Kaleidoscope.

When Robby received distributions from years saving taxes in what he understood to be a retirement savings plan it arrived as a cheque for thirteen hundred and thirteen loonies. Robby placed the amazing booby prize in a picture frame above the MOB's hundred-thousand loonie demand note written in the hand of his accountant, Al Fudgit.

Robby's allegations were ignored as outrageous: that a bank colluded with third parties in a predatory lending scheme that despite convincing evidence of misrepresentations, falsifications and breach of bank protocol bordering on criminal negligence any judge could see, the MOB sued ten years to collect alleged indebtedness to an undocumented loan secured by a photocopy of a promissory note.

Robby told Gofa his forensic audit would be part of the story.

Robby didn't know the scope of the tax-shelter scheme. Like many he couldn't believe Confoundation banks were capable of doing what the news said banks did in other places. Despite evidence of fraud the MOB made their case with supreme confidence and serious intent.

It was years later Robby discovered a commingled note for another loan in joint names with Bobbie. It was a tipping-point triumphant moment. He had good reason to buy a longer frame to hang the second note below the first, as a trophy from the spoils of law.

He told Gofa he would write another book.

People said Robby was 'Investor Zero' but he wasn't the first, there were millions before him. As time went by, more and more investors and even banks tumbled into spiraling debt crises of their making in the wake of greed and sleazy kickbacks to the likes of Phil Morrsacs.

The difference between Robby and other duped investors was that Robby saw it as a system. When the MOB wrote him he owed them more than he could ever have afforded to buy the house he lived in, he knew it had to be a scam. Robby saw through it as a brilliant game, and he wanted to know the rules so he could ask a judge for a trial.

Gofa's forensic audit was done and he told a plausible story that many believed, including Robby who wrote and published it in a book he called *The Perfect Sting*. A television studio called him for an interview and Robby explained he was a victim simply telling a story from his experience with lawyers and accountants. The producer suggested Gofa Beers join the interview to add an expert's point of view.

Robby was surprised a television producer was interested in his book. He figured it was more the topic of banking than praise for the author.

The media was full of stories of corruption and fraud and scams of all kinds. A government inquiry into misspent advertising money was the flavor of the month. There was a report, and then a trial that handed out a wicked deterrent to a convicted criminal. In lieu of two years' jail, a judge sentenced the mastermind to a community service lecture tour to teach business ethics to university students. The first, possibly the only reported muck master's class started with students taunting "Professor Scam! Professor Odd Scam!" in a skirmish at the door.

Robby sounded good on radio. He called in to live talk shows. It was a quirk of fate that allowed Robby to ask his question on a television broadcast of an election campaign... Robby was the first on hold.

"Our first caller is Robby. You are on the air..."

"Thank you. If the candidates knew of a 'Sitting Duck' scam that tricked people into tied loans with investments, would they side with public awareness, or bank profiteering?"

Three of four candidates agreed, one said, "We know the caller and have seen his van that expresses his indignation about banks. 'Tied Loans' are illegal, public awareness would be our priority of course."

But the question exposed a stark reality of government inaction...

For the first time a politician Robby had written several times before had to say something about the issue. *Finally*, an answer was required. To explain why writing the Confoundation and complaining to more than twenty agencies had been a complete and utter waste of time.

The incumbent was the last to speak and stood alone, being totally noncommittal about regulating banks. "I also know this case. And, I've been to the Finance Committee about the issue. There is nothing we can do, but let me add... our banks are among the finest in the world."

Having been a voice on a television phone-in, Robby was ready for a live interview. People would see him in person. The producer phoned to confirm Gofa would be there and told him how to get a security pass and when to meet him at the news desk.

Robby was more relaxed than the program producer might have expected. The anchor prophetically introduced the topic as a 'Debt Dilemma' with Robby as the author of an important book. It was easy, all he had to do was answer questions, the first being, "What made you write your book?"

He told the story of what happened and the interviewer asked Gofa, "How many times do you hear stories like Robby's?"

"Far too many, unfortunately. Since the late '80s, quite a few. I'd say well over two to three hundred a year."

Robby didn't think about it at the time... two to three hundred a year.

Now that's an interesting thing for a CFP to admit on television. Let's do the math, say: twenty years inclusive, middling two hundred and fifty a year. One each business day! With an average debt of eighty thousand using this venture as a good bad example.

$$20 \times 250 \times 80{,}000 = 400{,}000{,}000$$

With interest that would be a billion. Other financial planners might know more. How many? Several billion? How much could it be?

A cool billion in Gofa's personal estimation... from undisclosed trick loans. That'd bring out a few complainers, wouldn't you think?

If each day a bank paid eighty thousand to third parties with notarized 'Signature Affidavits' that loonies wanted to borrow to invest?

Robby isn't quick with numbers. He couldn't do the math to make the point on television, he was just excited to see his *Perfect Sting* book on screen with another question, "How did it start?"

"The book started when they called me a 'Sitting Duck'. The lawyers told the story. All I had to do was write what was happening, where the evidence came from, and government responses to my letters."

"Like a diary?"

"Yes, but very difficult. You can't imagine the anger over this. They blame me. The bank calls me a 'Sitting Duck' and a sophisticated investor at the same time. On my side it's tough to find a lawyer that hasn't got a conflict of interest, or isn't afraid of banks. They don't want these cases. I've heard of double-dealing lawyers who are on side with banks to make sure people can't win. Victims are abused and legalized to death. They give up, or go crazy. It's all in the book."

"How long did it take you to write it?"

"This one took three years. I'll write another after the trial."

"Do you think you'll get your money back?"

"They tell me it's a clear case of fraud I can't possibly win."

"So why are you fighting it?"

"I can't pay them. I didn't have credit for a loan to invest and I don't have credit now. They know I can't pay but they sue me anyway. Isn't it crazy? If these allegations ever went to court and a ruling came down against them there'd be a public outcry with catastrophic consequences for banking. They have to have to keep it quiet and ruin me the same as other people with trick loans. They take houses and garnish pensions and I've heard of suicides. The MOB is the biggest player; they have billions in notes. But, for me it's all about self-respect. I don't want to be a 'Sitting Duck'. I need an apology."

"Is that what it's all about?"

"Oh yes, they don't understand. We've lost way more than money." The camera caught a hopeless grin, and the interviewer said nothing.

 Then Robby said, "We didn't come here for this. We can't let banks give our money to third parties using improperly witnessed manufactured notes brought out to collect by litigation years later. It should to go to trial. But, what people really need is consumer safeguards proposed in Petition 44 for an inquiry into predatory lending practices."

After the broadcast people called their MP's about Petition 44.

At the time people were ignorant about ABCP Third Party Note credit default swaps. Complex derivatives were just finding their way into money markets as exotic financial instruments not widely known outside banking fraternities. It would take years and serious upsets before irresponsible lending with credit default swaps became a world credit crunch in double figures with twelve zeros.

On reflection, and knowing what people know today, it's just possible Gofa didn't have all the facts. There was more to the story than in his report that only scratched the surface. It was that, or a whitewash.

Robby thought L'Æmori and his cronies might have knobbled Gofa. It seemed likely when he gave evidence to help the bank.

Who'd know? Innocent or not, Gofa endorsed a non-arm's-length deal that sold tax shelter property to Kaleidoscope as the agent of the bank holding papered notes that took five million loonies off the sale price in a wicked parting shot. It's called a haircut in the trade.

It all seemed so long ago. The weave of time provided another surreal déjà-vu moment when Gofa and Robby met once again for a tell-all lunch and a beer. When they returned to the office Gofa handed him the complaint file returned to him from the Conjurer.

"This is what we sent Securities on Kaleidoscope," he said.

If Robby had any doubts that Gofa reported the crime to the authorities, they all but disappeared. The file was far more than he expected. Gofa handed him three volumes in considerable detail as clear testimony to lots of work done in good faith. So it seemed.

Gofa flipped through the pages to explain the table of contents, saying, "They told me we didn't have enough evidence to show any criminal intent. They think it's a civil matter. A civil matter," he said with disdain, "that's the Confoundation for you." He looked at Robby. "They won't see anything wrong in this."

He turned more pages. "Nothing wrong!" he said as he found what he was looking for. Gofa stabbed a finger into pages full of names and addresses. "All these people know it's wrong," he said pointing, but Robby couldn't make anything out in his eyes from where he sat.

Gofa found one. "This man won't talk to me… and see here, this lady calls me every day to tell me she blames me for losing her money."

He looked at Robby. "I'm fed up with Kaleidoscope, they need a comeuppance someday."

Their eyes fixed, and Gofa realized it was the bank leading the battle against Robby Ducky, so he added, "Them, and the MOB."

Gofa found a file-box for the binders Robby tucked under his arm with the box resting on his hipbone to take the weight. Like a mother carrying a child. He left the office and wondered what the heck to do with it… now he had scoop on the MOB for whatever the use of.

Unknown Unknowns

After the television interview, Robby had a word with his lawyer about it. They agreed better regulations would be good for consumer protection, but Robby didn't know what he could do to make the Confoundation more aware of the urgent need to control banks. It wasn't right, lawyers notarizing signatures for 'Sitting Duck' loans.

Robby's lawyer advised the case would interest an MP. His legal advice switched to political opinion that a new House Martin with a background in finance as a minister might have a sympathetic ear. He suggested Robby send his analysis to the government to follow up.

Robby had written complaints with a report that described the bank's 'Off-site Loans Closings' as a predatory lending scheme. He had a copy and was riled enough to send it to the government that very day.

When he got home he made a phone call. It was a Friday afternoon and the office secretary asked him to get the report to them as soon as possible. The MP was interested and Robby wrote a covering letter that he delivered personally with a few words to help it on its way.

It was only a couple of weeks before he heard from his MP. There was a message on the answering machine to press the play button:

> Yes! Hello, I'm calling on behalf of your member of parliament. And I'm just calling to let you know that we have received your file and we are, er, investigating it. I know that you requested a private member's bill be introduced on the issue, but we don't feel that a private members bill is the right way to go because they go into a lottery and they're only drawn a couple of times a session. There's just a very low chance it will be drawn out. We've actually taken this to the minister and various representatives at the Bankers' Association. And we're kind of investigating it, once we get some information about this issue we'll get back to you.

Robby played it again with his hopes rising. He made a note of the caller's name and telephone number. He was grateful for the apparent support, but in several weeks the outcome was disappointing. It was another message that simply closed the file: "We asked the bank about your allegations, and they say they don't do it anymore."

"The MOB doesn't do it anymore," Robby repeated out loud. He sat quietly just staring at the telephone a while.

That was all the Confoundation would say about the issue. As time went by Robby felt it wasn't good enough. He wrote a follow-up question after talking to Gofa, who said, "Why don't you ask them to identify the amended section in the Bank Act? That would tell you if they regulate what they appear to have done in the past."

A review of the Bank Act would prove if banks were regulated or not.

It was a good question for public debate. Good enough for Robby to be nominated to campaign for consumer safeguards in an election. He was perhaps the most visible defendant in Court and underreported election candidate in Confoundation history.

Reporters interviewed Robby and took pictures of him, even in his van on the way to Court, and also on the hustings. None of it made the news, and his association with political party leaders that signed Petition 44 for an investigation into bank lending practices was never reported.

While the Confoundation gave the appearance of interest in Robby's case, the establishment pushed back with relentless indifference. He reported the scam to the police three times. He wrote to dozens of complaint-handling agencies that ignored him with standard thank you rejection letters, others acknowledged it, and then advised they had no jurisdiction, or wouldn't or couldn't do anything about it.

Robby wrote the MOB about a blank loan application before the Court in the bank's Affidavit of Documents. It was strange they included an incriminating blank application for another loan. But, there it was, and being void he asked the bank to return or cancel it, so it couldn't be used to create another promissory note in his name.

But it was too late. Robby didn't know a bank employee had already filled out a demand note to sell him another derivative.

Robby was victim to unknown unknowns.

Robby's didn't know a note as yet unknown was commingled with the note known in litigation with the bank claiming an unknown note did not exist, as the unknown note was only known to the bank.

Robby wrote the House Martin about the blank bank loan asking the Confoundation to prevent the MOB creating a debt in his name and to protect others from similar loans tied to tax shelter sales. He requested a 'Sitting Duck' Private Members Bill for consumer protection.

Robby wrote a storybook, *The Perfect Sting,* to make his letters to the bank and the government not so easy to ignore.

But everyone ignored everything. It made no difference; the MOB was bent on collecting its note. The new House Martin didn't answer Robby's letters and did nothing about so-called 'Sitting Duck' loans. Everyone said it was a figment of his imagination that he made up as a conspiracy theory to avoid paying debt in his name.

Robby felt compelled to continue writing as he made his way through a legal quagmire. He wrote a motion for the Court to dismiss the bank's claim given their own witness identified the second note in examination. Robby filed an amended Factum of unknown unknowns he felt sure would compel a judge to rule in favour for a trial.

But blocking evidence was an unexpected unknown. It wasn't easy to get evidence past judges that said the law was clear that banks could collect money on the strength of photocopies of signed notes.

Clear or not, Robby wanted to know why the Gallows Prosecutor let him suffer the uncertainties of litigation for so many years without intervening in a matter reported as potentially criminal. Why hadn't the House Martin done anything about Petition 44 that people of the Great Divide and leading politicians signed for an investigation into predatory lending practices? Why wouldn't the Conjurer of Securities reopen a quashed file? What was so difficult about a Private Members Bill for a Responsible Lending Act that might settle financial markets not just in Confoundation, but around the world?

People might never know the dark secrets of banking, of dream laws and politics for hungry bankers unless they read the story. But if they were anything like judges, they probably wouldn't believe it.

Upon my Word

Al put the glossy brochures and contracts in his briefcase. He counted protruding 'Sign Here' tabs. He was on his way to see two prospects for Kaleidoscope tax shelters. One was a university professor and the other a restaurateur a couple of blocks from his office. They both had issues about tax, even complexes due to his accounting methods.

The professor scheduled a meeting in his lunch hour as the only free time he had for his accountant. The university was about a forty-minute drive in another car to satisfy Al's alter ego. A jet-black sports coupé with deep pile tan leather seats. Very sleek. Very smooth, and very quiet. He was in the mood for driving. Vroom, vroom.

Cory loved it, as did her sister, Fran. Fran said she wanted to buy it when he was done with it. They both knew how he was with cars.

Al parked his car across spaces for two cars and walked towards the university main entrance. His client was waiting for him in the lobby and they walked a corridor to a large refectory converted to a modern food hall with cafeteria walkways and various specialty menu outlets.

They parted ways along different aisles to choose food and rejoined at the cashier. Al paid and then honed in on a round table in a dark and relatively quiet corner. He carefully put his briefcase on a chair, and shuffled over to another beyond to sit face-to-face to the professor opposite Al with his back to the wall. The two of them ate and chatted about their busy lives and impossible work schedules.

After eating lunch the medical professor looked at his watch and said, "I haven't much time. I have a lecture theatre scheduled at one."

"That's all right, we only need signatures," Al said as he reached into his open briefcase to lift out a set of papers from the top. "Okay," he said, "all you have to do is sign and I'll fill out the details to see if you qualify for tax credits. Kaleidoscope will check it over and I expect you'll get the tax break we talked about."

"Well that's what it's all about," the other said with feeling.

"Mmm," Al sounded sympathetic as he placed the papers on the table.

Al smiled his pearly grin. "We'll do better than last year," he said. "If you're approved… I think it'll be a complete tax break for you. It's such a good deal. There's no risk. You get it all back in taxes."

"Look, it's time to go. I've got to get ready to operate."

Al said, "Right, I'll tell you where to sign." He stood up and began to fold pages away to reveal signature lines for the professor to sign with a pen he handed to him. It was a fine instrument and the professor looked at it for a moment before he signed on the first line with a sign-here Post-it next to a large red dot. Al lifted pages one by one until he had all the signatures he needed to close the sale.

He took the package and sat down and flipped through it to check it for a moment. Then he turned a page to look for something and said, "You have to initial here…" he paused as the professor did as he was told, "and here…" he pointed for another. "There, we're done." He took his pen and signed a different page.

"I have to go now, is that all there is?"

"Yes, that's all we need."

"Is it the right thing?" the professor said wondering.

"Believe me, it's perfect for you," said Al. "I'll take care of everything, I'm sure you'll get the tax benefit you need."

The professor looked at Al and then at his watch and said, "I have to dash, there's never enough time for anything personal these days."

They stood up. The professor was already thinking of what he had to do. He was looking and heading for the door as their hands touched in a limp handshake that quickly parted. Al watched him go.

He had done the job in twenty minutes, chatting and eating. Signing? He figured signing took a couple of minutes. Al knew he was good and it was getting easier for him all the time. He figured the professor would have forgotten all about it by the time he reached the door.

Al was in no hurry; he finished his coffee and lifted his open briefcase from the chair to the table. He put the papers into a hanging folder in the lid and closed it. He patted it fondly, picked it up and walked to the door. Then out to his car for what was on his mind… driving.

When Al got back to his office he put the professor's file into a folder containing similar legal papers. They were stapled neatly in stiff cardboard document corners. He noticed work to do in his in-tray and started another client's company books. He worked quietly. It took about an hour and he printed out a couple of copies before he was satisfied with the numbers.

When he was done, he took the document to his assistant and asked her to check it over for any errors she could see, and make the usual copies with a standard covering letter and disclaimers.

Al stopped at the water cooler going back to his office. He took a sip from a paper cup and threw it into the bin on the floor. Then he returned to his desk and picked up the phone and pressed a button to dial a number. "Granmarfleas," a young voice jested.

"This is Al Fudgit, is Jon Peair Fussy there?" He waited but the youth came back to the phone and told him, the main man, JP was busy and would get back to him.

"No. Tell him Al Fudgit has his yearend reports. I need a signature and I'll be there in a few minutes."

He was over minutes. The restaurant was just down the street, about three blocks. When he strode in with his briefcase in hand he could see how busy the place was. Several tables had been pulled together for a group he recognized from Lynchem investment brokers across the street. He approached Peair's wife, Maria, taking orders that he interrupted to ask her to let JP know he was there for signatures.

Maria served her tray, and then took another order. In a few minutes she returned to give Al a coffee. She said JP would be out to see him as soon as he could. She looked around and pointed for him to sit at an empty table in a quiet area from where they had borrowed tables and chairs to set up a banquet arrangement for the investors group.

Al drank his coffee and waited with his papers ready to sign until the restaurateur came over to see him. JP smiled and said, "You couldn't have picked a busier time than this."

Al chuckled. "It's got to be good for business. All I want is a couple of signatures to close the year, and then back to work," he grinned.

Ten years later, for the life of him, JP couldn't remember signing a note for a loan. He must have, but he couldn't remember. The lawyer collecting debt for the MOB wanted to know, shaking it in the air, "You signed the bank app and the note, huh? Didn't you read it?"

It was the same with Robby who couldn't recall exactly how or when. And Bobbie couldn't remember signing a note for the MOB either. The dates on the contract didn't help. It made no sense to Robby as he had receipts showing he worked out of town the day he was supposed to have signed an application for a loan one day, the contract the next.

Al left the restaurant walking briskly to hurry to his office and drop the financial instrument into a manila folder with more the same. He locked up, and left with a cheery word to his assistant saying good night, and that he would see her in the morning.

That evening he thought about bank loan applications. The professor would be a cinch with regular income with a house and only a small mortgage. The restaurateur would be easy as well. Robby's would be more difficult. He knew Robby had a mortgage with retail banking on his house, and a commercial line of credit that funded the business. Renovations helped. The property was obviously worth more than he'd paid for it a few years ago. Al slept on the problem, and in the morning he made an early start to make Cory's sales by accounting.

There was nobody around when Al turned up, and the first thing he did was make a fresh pot of coffee. It was 'the early bird rule' and communal office users expected it. He took a cup to his office and put it down while he unlocked his filing cabinets and desk drawers.

He found Robby's file and took out the application the bank wanted filled out with financial information. He knew he wouldn't get it right the first time but he was used to worksheets. That's what they were. He took a photocopy to make a draft and fuss about with numbers.

Al sat down and picked up a rubber-tipped pencil. He began to chew on it pensively. He'd prepared company books for years and he knew Robby had a good cash flow. They had followed his advice to record house improvements as a project using money from the company.

At the end of each year, Al identified personal and company expenses to calculate how much income they should take from a shareholder's loan account to 'pay back' personal items and balance the books.

That was the theory. It was math Al started when he became their accountant. Robby didn't really understand it. He was more used to a regular income with tax deductions at source. This was a different approach, but he trusted Al when he told them it was easier than wages and deductions. Al calculated how much they needed and wrote up payroll journal entries to add 'spent money' to annual books and income tax returns. The renovations were expensive and they reported that year's improvement costs for their highest income ever.

The Duckys had been in business about five years and the unusual peak triggered a Confoundation audit. At first Robby didn't mind, he thought someone would come and check how things were going. He naïvely expected advice and encouragement. The auditor must have thought him an idiot. Sequesters are only measured by what they can get. Business advice doesn't come from people bent on tax collection.

The auditor sat with the company books for five days and helping himself to coffee and free sandwiches for lunch. It seemed expected. The Prime Compounder wanted loonies and the auditor found them in the numbers. He calculated a lower business versus living space ratio and readjusted the operating costs and tax allowances accordingly. The difference was enough to justify the auditor's visit.

At the end of the week Robby owed the government about thirteen thousand in taxes, which Al said he could pay with a company cheque, as he would cover it later from dividends. The auditor wrote a report with instructions authorizing Al to log the penalty to the shareholders' loan account. Al said it wasn't too bad, so Robby thought it best to leave it between him and the Sequester… and forget it.

Robby had had enough of Confoundation audit experience; he just wanted to get back to taking care of business.

As ignorant and disinterested as he was, Robby didn't know Al set the stage for his own agenda, and the Confoundation with a plan to come back three years down the road, for an even bigger bite.

To Al the reassessment was an opportunity. After a while when things settled down, he approached the Duckys about wealth management and how to reduce personal income tax. This was the Kaleidoscope presentation. Al focused on tax avoidance as though it were essential. "You have to realize it's better to work and have an income that can be taxed. It means you have more money. The trick is to stop your loonies going to the taxman." Bobbie didn't really buy into the idea.

Robby didn't understand it either. He was noncommittal, but he didn't actually say "No". He rarely said "No" to anyone.

Yes or no didn't matter to Al who simply got as many signatures as he could to sell MOB loans. All he needed was personal identity and credit information. In Robby's case credit was the problem. There was none: it was all spent. Al knew they had taken out a company line of credit on the house. He figured office renovations increased personal net worth. If he showed company assets as personal and if the MOB ignored company debt... he could make it look good for Robby.

Al had already filled out loans for the professor and restaurateur with only minor deviations from reality. He padded the numbers with more in the assets column than in liabilities. Having done it once, he was in the mood to work on Robby. He thought about the man and the fun life he was having consulting jad – whatever! Al smiled to himself. Who said accounting was dull? He was gambling with people's livelihoods. It was a risk and a challenge. He could be a hero. It gave him a thrill.

He leaned back in his office chair and stared at the ceiling. He figured numbers that might work while he chewed the eraser thoughtfully. Al smiled as he balanced the round shaft lightly between a steady thumb and twitching forefinger to make it bounce between his teeth. It was a habit. He didn't mind the sound of wood drumming in his head, the same as a dentist makes checking for cracked molars. He was still smiling when he sat bolt upright and twirled the instrument round to start writing. He pressed hard as he put his machinations on paper.

He didn't stop writing until it was done. Then he sat back to read it.

There really wasn't much to it... personal details about Mr and Mrs Ducky; their address, his SIN – Social Insurance Number. He inflated loonies threefold and put the house at half a million with equity in the company at another quarter million. He wrote –NIL – for liabilities. Then he wrote a memo to Bobbie to add generous management fees to the payroll journal to pay government deductions by remittance. Next, he showed joint incomes at about a hundred and fifty thousand. Al knew he could show such numbers on their tax returns once he converted reconstruction costs in the shareholders' loan to wages.

The trap was set. Mr and Mrs Robby Ducky were rich, even on their tax returns that he could fill out after the Kaleidoscope deal.

Al worked hard for his referral fees. It seemed he'd been at it a long time. But it was still early, and the others were just coming in as he put the paperwork aside. He left his office for another cup of coffee.

Yul Perysh turned up, Al poured coffees and they chatted a while in the kitchen. They were still there when Al's assistant arrived and the accounting work-a-day routine started the way it always did. Al sent Bobbie a payroll adjustment memo on September 5th, and told her to report pension and tax deductions on schedule by the 15th.

Kaleidoscope guidelines told Al what next for the bank. He had just done 'Step One' and he smiled as he read the other steps. Getting all the documents signed at once meant 'Step Two' and 'Step Three' were done in one. All the bank needed, 'Step Four - the promoter is to complete Affidavit of Subscribing Witness', had to be done before he sent them in. He knew he had to wait... Mykle was still working with the MOB to underwrite another project. Al knew they couldn't handle anything until the contracts were signed for Kaleidoscope to operate as a bank with 'Off-site Loans Closings'.

Al was keen to find out if they were ready and he needed to gloat a bit. He called Mykle and left a message, "It's Al, I made three sales last week, I want to send you loan packages, um, give me a call and let me know when you're ready to process the eighty-nine."

He didn't have to wait long, the bank agreed to bankroll Façade on September 13th when Mykle went to Cyn's office to pick up the bank's 'Off-site Loans Closing' authorization to handle third party loans.

With funding arrangements and BWAB operations under way, Mykle sent a memo to salespeople to let them know he was ready to receive investment agreements and loan applications for the eighty-nine.

When Al read the memo, he knew what to do. He swiveled his chair to face his credenza to find the files he wanted. He wrote *September 18th* on Robby's 'Statement of Affairs' and sent it to Kaleidoscope.

The next day, Al signed the bank's 'Affidavit of Subscribing Witness' form in the MOB's appendices Robby had already signed. He only had to witness it and get a Notary Public to notarize it with a date, place and seal of office as a 'Taker of Affidavits'. It was a common practice in accounting. He'd done it before, and he knew a lawyer to call to notarize it for him to make his oath legally binding.

He picked up the phone and pressed a number in memory. "Hi… it's Al." They chatted for a few minutes and then he said, "I've a couple of affidavits, It'll only take a minute… sure, eleven o'clock then."

Al had to get the bank documents ready. He fed Robby's 'Affidavit of Subscribing Witness' into a typewriter and typed in the location and date, September 19th, on the next line. He had just done it when the phone rang. He turned his chair to answer it. "Al Fudgit," he said.

"It's Mykle, I've got a loan application from Robby Ducky and I want to know when you're coming in with the contract?"

"Hi," Al said cheerfully, "Okay, I can bring it in just as soon as I've had a lawyer sign the affidavit."

"What? Ah yes, that's something I do here, right? You have to bring it in for to me to notarize it," Mykle said in a menacing tone.

Al didn't catch on. "You have a Notary in your office?" he inquired.

"Yes!" Mykle snapped. "I told you, G'damn it's in the sales manual."

Al thought about it quickly, and said, "I should come now, eh?"

"That will do just fine, I'll buy lunch." The mean edge had gone and Mykle spoke more easily. "It's a nice day, get in your shiny car, and bring in those sales contracts, the sooner I see them the better."

The idea of lunch with Mykle sounded good to Al, and he picked up his sales and put them in his briefcase. Then he trotted out of the office to satisfy his endless passion for driving cars.

They met about eleven-thirty and Al apologized that he'd forgotten Mykle was a Commissioner of Oaths.

"I was a lawyer with Ardent Bailiffs," Mykle said. "I don't practice but I can still take affidavits. It's my job to see these deals through."

He looked at the bank's form. "You've got the wrong location. I'll have to change it." He typed Xs through it, and 'Ogstowne' above it. Then he scrawled his signature and stamped it, and said, "That's it, it can go to the MOB, and we can go to lunch." He looked happy.

It amused Al to see Mykle sign affidavits without trepidation. Just a cursory review to check bank material properly signed and dated as required to set up and collect trick loans. No question of preference to swear an oath, a hand upon a book of faith, or his heart in solemn declaration. Nothing: Al felt it was just a prerogative to do business.

Mykle stamped affidavits for people's signatures with a lawyer's zeal to steal, but that was all. He simply checked it and signed it. Debtors making notes had no idea. They were uninvolved, unaware and never saw the money. Taking identity affidavits was a sacred ritual between the bank and its agent. Aside from getting signatures Al had no reason to be there, and he took to swearing for Mykle over the phone.

It was the same for all salespeople that swore to a deity people wanted to borrow money to invest in debt sold as retirement savings plans.

When questioned in congress, bankers swore they did God's work.

Al waited for his boss to get his coat to walk outside that was chilly. He opened the door as Mykle still spoke on topic. "You have to send all the MOB's Affidavits of Subscribing Witness to me to notarize. The fewer lawyers know about it, the better. Anyway, I don't suppose you want to pay their fees." He smiled and quipped, "Who knows, this way you might even sell one to a lawyer. He he ha hah."

They both smiled at the strange possibility and set out for lunch.

Mykle and Al got on well in each other's company. They had similar views as far as getting money was concerned. They'd do anything to lay their hands on it. Mykle also found Al a good listener as he talked about his plans to acquire more property.

"We have 'Hilltop Lace' in the Rookies. It'll be the first ninety for next year," Mykle said. "It's a smaller venture out west. You can sell it to lower income earners, or clients that could save more tax."

"Is the MOB funding it?" Al inquired.

"They're the most involved in SIV markets. All they need from me is notarized signatures. They're our best choice for our client loans. We have a few things to sort out, but it'll be ready in a few weeks."

Investment bankers and the Prime Compounder recommended people save tax money to buy tax sheltered property for retirement income. Mykle was as prolific creating schemes as Al was selling them, even before they were announced. He had leeway with clients that trusted him the way they did. They didn't have a clue what they were getting into. Only the banks and their agents knew the rules of the game.

Al recommended a ninety to Robby to balance his portfolio. He said, "You have more income this year and could do with the saving."

Again there was no mention of cost. Al showed Robby the immediate effect of Façade. "See how it works, there's no cost. Why give money to the taxman when you can own property at government expense? All you have to do is sign tax shelters." He did the math on Robby's tax return to demonstrate the benefit to close another sale.

Yearend sales were a bit of a hassle and to save time Al didn't bother to fill out a tax creditworthy statement of affairs for the ninety loan.

It might have been that Al forgot the bank used the same document to assess credit for people to borrow to invest. Robby didn't know the role of the bank, or that he would get a loan when he signed the ninety contract, any more than he knew about for the eighty-nine before.

People might think banks would be more careful about undocumented loans that generally passed for sloppy banking in the trade.

Robby wasn't the only one. The game required investors to sign blank notes for tied loans in the deal. Al was a member of the local Rotation Club where he held meetings to peddle Kaleidoscope tax shelters. There were other sales reps, but Al was the most successful temporary bank employee witnessing signatures for loans that paid his fees when he filled out bank credit decisions on promissory notes that closed sales.

He even sold one to his wife Cory. Al had her sign a promissory note to owe the MOB knowing they would want to collect it one day. He grinned to himself as he submitted Cory's app for another referral fee.

It was a quickie and he wondered if the MOB would process a note more difficult to collect than others, the way they skimmed loans. They did, and when it came time for the bank to sue the Fudgits, Al called his trusty lawyer Mewkus Clayman to fight it out in court.

Al was also rewarded with sales meetings in a private baseball box at Wodgers stadium. When he made a sale to a politician and a lawyer it was cause for celebration. It was a hoot, Mykle showed Al's notes to Marion, and they chuckled as he notarized one after the other.

The bank was happy. Smiles all round as Mykle brought in a windfall of tied loans. He notarized loony's names for the MOB that sent him loonies in return. Phil Morrsacs advised the Board of Directors to repeat the plan for more ABCP projects. Mykle became a celebrity with invitations to speak at business schools and cocktail parties.

He would tell his little joke about how much money he was making.

Accounting Scripts

It was almost three years to the day when the Sequester called Bobbie advising there was another audit due. This time they explained Robby and Bobbie borrowed money from their company to pay their own salaries. So, they would have to pay a deemed interest penalty at current rates of interest, which in the eighties and early nineties reached seventeen percent the government charged in the last audit.

They figured Robby Ducky owed about sixty thousand in back taxes.

Robby couldn't understand it and wanted to know how it could have happened. The accounting explanation was as creative as anything he'd ever heard. Paying the previous audit penalty produced a retroactive negative balance recalculated through past years. As such, the line of credit paid wages from money borrowed to cover operating expenses. It depended how you cooked the company books. Robby pointed out he always earned enough to cover his wages.

The auditor said, "That's true, but you also had to pay your staff and business expenses. They come first, so there's nothing left to pay your own salaries… the tax penalty you paid from the shareholders' loan account did it. It looks as though you borrowed from yourself."

"But I invoice my time. I always get paid less than the invoice, how can you say I had to borrow from myself to get paid?" Robby pleaded with Al who sat next to the auditor across the table.

"You have operating expenses all the time, including interest charges, cash flow goes negative sometimes," Al explained. "If there's nothing left you have to borrow from the company. That's the way they hit you with a deemed interest on personal taxes."

"But my work for clients brings in the money."

"Doesn't matter," the auditor said quickly.

Robby thought. "Look, the way I see it, the company cash flow didn't actually go negative until you created a thirteen-thousand loony reassessment, three years ago. You made us pay more tax, right?"

"Right," the auditor said without expression.

"And previous to that everything was positive. I mean real, we had real money on the books to pay wages?"

"Yes."

"Then you told us to backdate a tax adjustment, and pay it from the shareholders' loan account, and the numbers we'd previously reported in positive cash flow got switched to negative. So, according to the new accounts we didn't have enough money to pay wages back then. Even though we did at the time." Robby found it hard to choose his words as he struggled with the almost impossible logic.

"Yes," the auditor repeated, "our figures show you borrowed income."

"So today you look at the numbers and tell me I have to pay sixty thousand loonies for a deemed benefit of borrowing, even though it wasn't actually borrowed at the time, not until we paid reassessed taxes. Now I have to pay three years' seventeen percent interest on a debt that never existed, all because in your interpretation I borrowed from myself to pay myself?" Robby knew it sounded as though he was babbling, but it must have made some sense to accountants.

"Not from you, the company," the auditor said.

"I earn money. It comes in when I work," Robby responded.

"Yes."

"Look, what if we challenge the reassessment, can we put the positive cash-flow back the way it was?" Robby pleaded.

"It's too late, you already paid. Why didn't you challenge then?" The auditor smiled at the struggle.

"Huh! That's easy," said Robby, "I just wanted to be rid of you. I didn't know faffing about with numbers would do this to us."

Nobody said a word until Robby spoke. "It's crazy. You're saying if our cash flow ever goes negative due to accounting, if Bobbie and I take income, it has a deemed interest which is a taxable benefit."

"I don't make the rules," the auditor said with a shrug. "I just work for the Confoundation."

"As I see it the government has a huge deficit. Does that mean every politician that gets paid should declare a deemed interest on their personal income tax until the deficit's gone?" Robby glared at them.

Al was hoping Robby wouldn't notice that the company's 'shareholders loan account' increased to pay Kaleidoscope loans from the business line of credit. He saw the paradox: "Hmmm… that's good Robby," he said. But the auditor said the simple truth.

"The Confoundation doesn't operate by the rules. It doesn't work that way. You have to pay us. You can't argue with the government."

Robby gave up. He'd exhausted all the reason he could muster. His head hurt, as did his heart. He knew it was the end of business as he knew it. The more he worked the more tax he had to pay. It was over.

In the weeks that followed, the auditor and Al agreed to a method of payment for such a large amount. The government sent them another letter to authorize Robby to borrow another sixty thousand from the shareholders loan account with instructions how to report it.

It sickened Robby. He had worked hard to be free of debt. He didn't like debt. He didn't know Al was the cause of debt in a huge tax bill generated by crazy interpretations of accounting rules.

Robby only knew he had to do what a lot of business people were doing. He had to fire everyone including himself, and take on people as independent contractors that send invoices for time and materials. It put an end to deemed interest on borrowing to earn a living. The company spirit was never the same again.

Robby's lifetime objective was to be debt-free. The audit was a body blow that left its mark. But in time, he rallied round and started over.

Robby and Bobbie did what they had to do to solve the problem. His generous nature came up with a perverse rationale. He figured it was the government's way of sharing the common wealth of hard working people. It was their way of giving to the less fortunate, more in need.

Jadding was fun for Robby, and he decided to work even harder.

Years later, after explaining it to a lawyer, "I think Al wanted me to have a tax problem," Robby lamented.

The lawyer agreed and said it didn't have to be done that way. "Your accountant could have declared it an executive perk on the company books. You could have put the money to much better use. You could have spent it on client entertainment for a government contract."

But that was a future hindsight yet to play into Robby's life. There was another. What he didn't know was that Al had set him up for an even bigger debt that he wouldn't know about for several years, when he should have been looking forward to a carefree retirement; a sometime 'Freedom fifty-five' is what they call it in the adverts.

Financial freedom was a question on many people's minds.

Robby was fifty-five when he discovered the trouble he was in. He found himself in a world of doom and gloom and political fearmongering at the turn of the century. Computers everywhere would crash on too many date-sensitive zeros, and stop the march of time.

But not so the endless march of corruption and corporate rip-offs… What had been once reported as merely several million loonies, the global credit crunch got bigger by three zeros, and then some…

Tax Credit Worthiness

Robby followed the computer log in court documents as though he were a fly on the wall watching the creation of debt in the making.

"Here's another application from Kaleidoscope."

"How does it look?" Cyn asked Sully as she handed him a printout from the CCAP – Credit Crunch Adjudication Process.

"It's OK, I guess. He has a good credit rating. He signed it, but she didn't, but I've calculated a TDSR on her income as well. You told me to do that, right? He has an expensive house, and no debts. Lucky devils. They've developed a business that pays them good dividends."

"What business?"

"Something about jad, whatever that is. He has a consulting practice. Regular cash flow, but not much in assets."

"Right, the income sounds okay, I'll mark it approved. Did it come in with a waiver and signature affidavit?" He referred to the second note.

"Yes sir." Sully knew which 'note' was he was talking about.

"Rubberstamped our note and PLSA?" he checked.

"Done." Sully handed it to him carefully. "It's wet, don't smudge."

The red ink glistened. "It's another from Al Fudgit, eh?" He looked at the signature affidavit. "Yep… thought so. He's good at this."

Cyn logged on to his computer, and opened the file using his personal password. He tabbed from the first entry and typed in details that started and updated an automatic log with the date and time. The new input was under the headings 'AC Misc' and 'Rte Comments'. He knew what they were. He typed a message and pressed the enter key.

13:13 REPRESENTS REFERRAL FROM KALEIDOSCOPE
TO A PURCHASE ONE UNIT OF PROJECT 89

Cyn looked at the loan application form and the financial information sheet, and continued typing into a computer log Teletype message format. It took a few minutes before he sent out his approval.

13:55 BASED ON OUR CLIENT TNW OF 580 M. TDSR AT 6%
EXCELLENT STABILITY AND JOB TYPE. EXCELLENT
CREDIT EVIDENCE BY BUSINESS BANKERS REPORT.
RECOMMEND 50,000 PDLT 12/300 P+1% J/S UNSECURED.
SUBJECT TO ANNUAL REVIEW. THANK YOU IN ADVANCE.
CYN FORDO.

Cyn felt good with three 'loan applications' from Kaleidoscope that morning and several in the system already. Red-stamped ink dried and everything was working tickety-boo. He tapped a tuneless ditty with his pen on a cup full of pens, and waited for the computer to respond. The first error message for credit alert turned up with a new code as the computer clock ticked through its thirteenth hour.

13:57 RECOMMEND INVESTIGATION

Cyn looked at the errors flagged. It was the first of nine alerts before he would be done. He had a lot of help. The computer did everything. It was quick and he didn't have to use real numbers. Anything would do. All he had to do was get loan transactions through the system.

The system accessed input data to produce a message and update the loan application log. The MOB knew more about the Ducky's than they knew about themselves. It was only a matter of moments before another CCAP error message turned up for Cyn to handle.

13:58 HITS 1

And a few minutes later, more credit alert flags and responses.

14:19 UNDECLARED 21,000 LIEN LOCATED AT MAIN BRANCH
14:21 ADDED UNDECLARED LOAN AND VISA
14:32 CONFIRMS LIEN IS TERM LOAN OF 46,000 AT 1540 MONTH
15:09 CYN, THERE SEEMS TO BE UNDECLARED LOAN, CALL CLIENT
15:14 UNABLE TO CONTACT ACC MGR. CANNOT CALL CLIENT

A Cyn full day ended when he signed off. He returned in the morning to find Sully looking at a report from a property search.

"This is what we got on the Ducky's," she said, and handed it to him. "Aren't these the people Al said had no debt?"

"Mmm," Cyn murmured and opened the manila folder to review the Statement of Affairs. He handed it to her to take a look.

"Well he didn't pay three hundred for his house he says he did. It says here it was only ninety-five and he assumed an existing first mortgage of sixty." She looked up. "It's way off, should we put a stop on it?"

"Not yet." Cyn put the report among the other pages of the file.

"He must really want to impress," Sully said with a chuckle. "Didn't the loony say his house was worth half a million?"

"It's OK. It's one of Al's clients. I'll call the accountant about it." A message appeared on the CCAP log while he was on the phone.

12:23 CYN, CAN'T FIND LNDG BR PLS ASSIST ADJUDICATE CREDIT

He saw the message and looked at the public records report again. As well as property details and the purchase price it listed two mortgages. There was sixty assumed in the purchase, plus a hundred in a second mortgage with the Tidy Bank. That's what Robby's credit flags were all about. "This is going to be difficult," he thought aloud.

The banker looked at the net worth and started to fill out the bank's PLSA. According to Cyn, Robby became a very wealthy man.

Al told Cyn Robby Ducky had three expensive cars, a house worth half a million, quarter million in company assets and a life insurance for two-hundred thousand plus seventy-thousand loonies in RRSP's.

The MOB figured Robby was worth a million, with no liabilities.

Robby, who was still paying seventeen percent interest on a line of credit to keep his business going, and now a chunk to pay off the Prime Compounder, would have wished it were true... a millionaire back then at forty-five. He would definitely have retired.

Cyn called Al to get more information on the Duckys.

13:57 UNDECLARED ASSET SOLD NET 50,000 AS PER ACC'NT

"Good. That would show the client had been sloppy filling out the loan application." At least that's what Cyn would say if he were ever asked. There are bound to be errors in declared assets and liabilities. Anyway, it was up to him to decide if the MOB should risk a loan. Cyn didn't think twice whether the Ducky's could afford it. He didn't care. Going to St Lucia was just a matter of approving loans.

On paper the Duckys were unlucky. Al boosted their joint income at yearend, his by sixty thousand to cover renovations, and hers by thirty thousand to pay the Prime

Compounder. If there'd been no company and no shareholders' account, there wouldn't be any dividends to pass spent money as income on tax returns. But Al did the accounting, and he always said, "I've made the numbers work."

The trouble was Robby's record keeping wasn't in the hands of one creative accountant. There were two more in line. The government had just taken a huge bite without anesthetic. Now, the MOB was poised to take another, with ignorance that kept Ducky unaware of a bleeding that remained internal for years to come.

Al didn't need to explain the Ducky's apparent high income to the MOB. The numbers were self-evident and reason enough for anyone to want, and obviously benefit from a tax shelter. So, the same way the government recalculated figures to tax deemed interest, the bank forced numbers for an undisclosed tied loan to close a sale.

But, the numbers still weren't good enough. Even for Cyn as anxious as he was for a trip to St Lucia. They were well below adjudication guidelines. The bank needed credit to advance funds to Kaleidoscope selling tax shelters. Cyn had to calculate another hundred thousand loonies for Robby Ducky to afford to buy a unit in Façade.

If Cyn used property search numbers as reported, Robby's net worth would be only half that required. He had to include Mrs Ducky's assets and income for it to be even close. She hadn't signed for a tax shelter or a loan, but she was married to a 'Sitting Duck' and that was good enough for Cyn to include her credit in the equation.

The reward system is a critical success factor for any Ponzi scheme. In this case it paid for an accountant to fudge the numbers, and for a bank officer to turn a blind eye to regulations with willful ignorance of credit alerts. Cyn disregarded exceeded thresholds and he used his override authority to advance the transaction through the system. He left forms blank in parts that should have been filled out to track a 'New Client Loan' with dates to see it through normal bank procedures, which should have included and recorded client contact.

When it came to record keeping, Cyn knew there was a difference between what he had on paper and in the computer. He also knew the only link was Al's 'Statement of Affairs' the bank's equivalent of a 'Loans Application'. It wasn't credible information. Indeed, with so many flags Cyn should have checked to find out more about Robby as the applicant, except that MOB 'Off-site Loans Closings' didn't need clients' signatures. The bank uses signature affidavits instead.

Years later, a lawyer told Bobbie the bank should never have calculated her into the deal, let alone use her credit information without her permission. "They broke a trust you had a right to assume. But they can claim they did nothing wrong, it was the accountant who gave it to them. You could sue them for professional negligence and wilful oversight of the facts. It would be a difficult argument, and all it would do is prove your husband, and hence you, were both victims. Robby's counterclaim will cover the financial impact, so you can't claim any financial loss. It would be very expensive and even if you won, there wouldn't be any money in it for you," he said.

Robby was amazed by the record, the number of times MOB people documented him a 'Valued Customer', while perpetrators that walked the talk, the 'Mechanics of Deception' called him a 'Sitting Duck'.

Cyn did all he could to divert attention from mortgage hits, which unlike 'Whac-a-mole' furry-heads popping up in a fairground hitting game, credit alerts that shouted "Boo" he never whacked at all.

Double or Quits

"Kaleidoscope, Façade Properties," the handset squawked.

"Mykle L'Æmori, please."

"Yes sir. Can I say who's calling?"

"Cyn Fordo, Osowega Branch."

"Yes sir, please hold… transferring you now, go ahead."

"Mykle L'Æmori here."

"Yes, Mykle, it's Cyn."

"How's it going?" Mykle knew the poor showing in sales and he half-expected a call. He figured he knew what it was about.

"Were getting through the loans you sent us, but we're short."

Mykle was worried about not making enough sales and said, "Al was at the Okivil Rotation Club last night and he got a couple of sales. One's a lawyer, puh." He didn't have much respect for family lawyers and professional rivalry came over in the tone of his voice. "We have another meeting at the Hambelton Rotation on Friday."

"Any prospects?"

"A few, we have our guns loaded." Mykle thought a moment. "We wrote people at the University Hospital and we have a reference from the faculty. Daveh will be there with Al to show the video and we've laid on food and wine. Al's helping new reps with their clients. Should be a few takers."

"Well Al knows how to close 'em," Cyn agreed with a chuckle.

"So we'll let you know." Mykle wanted to get on.

There was a click and a voice came over: "Mykle it's Bræn here."

Mykle realized he was on a speakerphone. "Hi Bræn."

"I'm thinking," said Bræn. "It looks as though we might have to drop the gig. I don't think you'll get enough buyers to close the offering."

Mykle was startled. It wasn't what he wanted to hear, not yet anyway. "We still have time," he said.

"Not enough in my experience," said Bræn.

"You're only just past fifty percent," Cyn added, sounding concerned.

"There's more to come, I've told you."

Bræn said, "Maybe if you got eighty percent we could double a few, you know, to make up the difference."

Mykle knew Bræn was right. It was a difficult market since the last bubble burst. "We'll have to talk about it. I'll call my reps for a blitz."

"You could let us know which you think are good for more," Bræn said seriously.

"More apps?" Mykle wondered what Bræn had in mind.

"No, we just need to know if we can qualify people for more units."

Cyn jumped in. "If you let us know which people are keen for more we can increase loan amounts in CCAP's. All the notes are blank. We just need you to fill them out when we daylight."

"Fill 'em out?"

"Yes, they're blank." Cyn wanted to increase sales to close the deal. "It's not like we have to fill out new apps. We just send notes back to you for your reps to fill out what their clients want to borrow."

Mykle thought of it differently. "We got your notes signed already. You make credit decisions, why don't you just fill them out?"

Cyn recalled Daveh's conscience; he didn't expect it in Mykle. "No, it's *your* sale. If you want us to go through with it, our notes have to look as though they were filled out and signed at the point of sale."

He emphasized who was the stakeholder. "Banks can't be seen to be involved in sales, so we can't fill out notes as though we were there."

He looked at Bræn for support as he spoke into the phone to make himself clear. "Can we?"

Mykle mumbled, "Don't suppose." Bræn nodded in agreement.

"Right," Bræn continued, "if you advise any changes we'll do what we can with punters' credit, then we'll call you how much to fill out."

"I'm sure it'll work out," Cyn said reassuringly. "We'll just wait here and see what comes. Okay?"

Mykle accepted the responsibility. "Alright, I'll be in touch."

There was nothing left to talk about and Mykle heard Cyn and Bræn in harmony, "Right, bye then," as the line went dead.

Cyn looked at Bræn and said, "What do you think?"

"I think we'll get more orders."

"Mmmm, betcha Al's the first one to double-take."

It was a pretty safe bet for a banker to make, knowing the game they were in and the players in it.

Cyn was busy ignoring credit alerts for Robby Ducky right up to the very last day of closings when Cyn received a memo from MOB Securities with a terse warning: 'Collateral Deficiency Notification'.

MOB Securities Department wanted an explanation about Robby's one hundred thousand mortgage, and signing irregularities.

Robby's loan application stated clear title that despite warning flags, Cyn refused to acknowledge Robby had a mortgage on his house.

Audit wanted to know why. Also, why had Robby signed a note with one pen, and initialed a change to it, supposedly at the same instant with another pen filled with different colored ink?

Cyn chose to ignore the mortgage on the deficiency notification. It was too late anyway. He was ahead in a CCAP 'Decision Summary' screen to enter amounts from bank calculations that Robby would have denied. Cyn forced the loan through with imaginary numbers: total assets of five hundred and eighty thousand and total liabilities of only eight thousand eight hundred for a net worth of five hundred and seventy-one thousand two hundred loonies. The exaggerations were good enough to approve an investment loan for fifty thousand loonies to close the sale of one unit. The computer confirmed the transaction.

The issue of a different colored pen to initial the note was due to a change of plan. Someone told Cyn, Robby wanted to buy two units.

14:35 FURTHER TO OUR ORIGINAL INPUT WAS INCORRECT.
MR. DUCKY WISHES TO PURCHASE 2 UNITS TOTALING 100,000. WE REVISED THE TOTAL TDSR WHICH REFLECTS TOTAL PAYMENTS INCLUDING OUR PROPOSAL OF 3,787 OR 18% PLEASE AUTHORIZE

Doubling the sale quantity would have been a problem if contract quantities and bank-demand note amount had been filled out when they were signed at the time of sale. Not so with MOB 'Off-site Loans Closings' that handled pre-executed loans completely backwards.

Getting signatures on blank bank notes and investment contracts provided enough flexibility for dealers to fill out quantities according to bank lending decisions. In closing, Al Fudgit filled out the bank's demand note for Robby for a hundred thousand to sell two units.

Other people weren't so lucky; several duped investors were sold up to four units according to promissory notes that sales reps filled out on their behalf. In the end Robby was sold three units including a ninety that depended on his creditworthiness for a trick loan. Instead of being overextended, the MOB calculated ownership in Façade as an asset in income producing property – the same value as the debt.

According to the MOB there was no carrying cost in Kaleidoscope tax shelter deals that made people rich and more creditworthy for debtors to borrow as long as they could claim and save tax credits.

On the Money

Cyn won his rhetorical bet when a message Robby wanted to buy another unit went into the CCAP system. But there was still a problem. In filling out Robby's bank's note for one hundred thousand loonies to sell two units, Al wrote a rate of interest that was incorrect and it had to be changed. The change on the note required initials.

Al wasn't the only sales rep confused about what the MOB wanted on blank promissory notes. All of them had to change 'Prime + 1%' as written to a figure on a line before printed text 'over prime'. The bank needed a decimal number to define how much interest to charge.

Aside from increasing amounts on demand-notes for people to borrow to invest, all the notes had to be initialed by all the clients agreeing to increased amounts and interest. Not an easy task. And no time to do it.

How could a bank get people to initial changes to red-rubberstamped and filled-out promissory notes without disclosing trick loans?

It was a setback. It made all the notes null and void. Cyn had to do something. He didn't mind being creative with CCAP numbers to force trick loans. His conscience didn't trouble much on that score. But messing with people's initials on notes was potentially criminal.

There were too many loonies in the game. Cyn knew he could justify debt the same as he knew judges would. If people signed blank notes the final amount was their own fault for being stupid.

He could live with court justification. But changing notes required drastic action, including forgery as the best option to solve a problem.

It wasn't unheard of: in a recent case before the IDA – Indifferent Dealers Affiliation the MOB had to pay a hefty deterrent fine of one hundred thousand loonies for signing signatures for the convenience of their clients. The wayward bank took a hit for the amount of Robby's loan. Cyn approved millions in trick loans. He knew his bonus depended on helping clients borrow money. It was his job.

He had to choose: forgery, or surprise letters asking clients to initial changes to promissory notes to evidence undisclosed bank loans.

There was no time for letters that would raise questions. Somehow, miraculously, all the bank's notes were initialed as required. It was a problem to MOB Securities that reported signing irregularities due to dissimilar pens with different colored inks as unusual at the time.

Among the amended notes, the MOB had one from Robby Ducky. The bank's lawyer relied on it when they sued him to repay it.

The amount was clearly filled out by Al who admitted it was in his handwriting but he denied forging initials. Robby couldn't remember seeing it being filled out, or initialing it, even though the style looked similar to his own. Al said a banker must have done it.

Robby denied he initialed it, but the judge didn't care.

Cyn didn't have to worry who initialed notes. They all turned up as required. It was what he wanted to close business. And, because the notes were the only things needed to make loans and collect debt, the documentation was ignored and remained the same as when it started.

In Robby's example the bank's PLSA for him to buy one unit wasn't changed to two. It wasn't signed. So it didn't matter.

Perhaps Cyn had no time to go back and double up the amount on the loan application. Or maybe he just forgot to do it after changing the borrowed amount in the computer that fed loonies to Mykle on the fateful day. All that mattered to Cyn was the computer that paid his bonus. To him, any closing was a good closing if it landed in debt.

More than likely it was Bræn Chyld's response to Cyn's eleventh-hour need to cover his backside. He wrote Audit a letter to stop them sending collateral deficiency notifications about signing irregularities.

Bræn had a good handle on compliance for which the Confoundation has a solid reputation of being the 'Wild West' in money markets.

He figured the MOB had no reason to fear signing irregularities at the time or even in court if it came to that. He was proven right; there wasn't a judge in Confoundation that found fault with tampered notes where even photocopies are good enough for banks to collect by litigation. No matter how incriminating or however long it takes.

Nine credit alerts, changed quantities and signing irregularities weren't the only problems in the bank's application for a loan for Robby.

Cyn checked the paperwork and rolled his eyes and cursed Al for not witnessing the agency waiver. But just as nine flags hadn't fazed him, he didn't think twice about signing witness and dating it himself. Without Robby ever knowing, and never being there… Cyn Fordo, Manager Executive Loans witnessed his journey into debt.

TO: A FREND DEC 1, 89
COMMUNITY BANKING MANAGER

RE: CHANGES TO KALEIDOSCOPE 89 BANK NOTES:

IT HAS COME TO MY ATTENTION THAT THERE MAY BE SOME CONCERN
OVER THE VARIOUS COLORS AND / OR PRINT OF THE BODY AND / OR
FIGURES OF KALEIDOSCOPE 89 LIMITED PARTNERSHIP DEMAND NOTES.

AS YOU ARE AWARE WE OBTAINED APPROVAL FROM CREDIT DEPARTMENT
ALLOWING OFF SITE CLOSINGS FOR THIS PACKAGE. THE UNITS FROM
THIS OFFERING WERE SOLD IN THE SELLING PERIOD WITH A TENTATIVE
CLOSING DATE, IF FINANCING WAS REQUIRED BY THE INVESTOR, THE DOCU-
MENTATION WAS SIGNED AND SUBMITTED TO THE MOB IN ACCORDANCE
WITH CREDIT AUTHORIZATION OF SEPT 13TH 89.

SINCE THE CLOSING DATE WAS NOT FIRM AT THE POINT OF SALE,
AND THE PRIME RATE NOT KNOWN, THE DATE AND PRIME RATE WERE
NOT COMPLETED ON THE DEMAND NOTE. IT WAS AGREED THAT THIS
INFORMATION WOULD BE COMPLETED WHEN THE CLOSING DATE WAS
ESTABLISHED, ALL OF WHICH WOULD BE CONFIRMED WITH THE CLIENT.

ON THE BASIS OF DISCUSSIONS WITH OPERATIONS / AUDIT, I AM
OF THE OPINION THAT THERE IS NO RISK ASSOCIATED WITH OUR
DOCUMENTATION AND AS SUCH WILL NOT PRESSURE THE PROMOTER /
AGENT OR CLIENT TO SIGN NEW DOCUMENTS.

BASED ON THE FOREGOING IT IS NOT NECESSARY TO REPORT THESE AS
COLLATERAL DEFICIENCIES.

BRÆN CHYLD

Cyn pulled out a 'New Account Record' and started filling it out with a date and account number and client 'Personal Summary' where he scribbled the 'Applicant' name as Robby Ducky with a half-million-dollar home equity. He didn't bother to read what he had seen many times in a 'Customer Agreement' sentence above signature lines that according to bank protocol should have been signed by the recipient debtor. 'I/we (the undersigned) agree to the terms and conditions as shown on the reverse of the following and acknowledge receipt of the Better banking Guide Personal Deposit Services.'

Paperwork was a nuisance to Cyn as he rushed his hand over the form with a swirl where a client's signature should have been. It looked like 'Cyn', but it didn't matter, his scribble was barely legible.

The words in the bottom right-hand corner indicated it was a receipt, '2 – Customer Copy' and across the middle in bold letters next to a bank logo, 'Thank you for banking at the MOB'. He put it in Robby's file and threw the customer copy into the waste bin.

Cyn looked at the Step Transaction checklist on the inside of Robby Ducky's folder and check-marked what he was supposed to do. He ticked 'Client Advised about Advancing Funds' as if he'd called, which he hadn't. "They can't prove I didn't call them," flitted through his mind. Check the 'Affidavit of Subscribing Witness' had the same date as the bank note, which it didn't. "How could it?" Cyn thought as he ticked 'Dealer Advised' and 'Confirmation Sent', and he left 'File BF for Future Solicitation?' Another sale? "Perhaps."

'Dealer Advised' happened twice for Cyn. Mykle the agent and Al the sales rep both called to make sure the MOB sold two units to Robby Ducky as requested. Cyn's phone rang while he was computing. "Cyn Fordo," he said. It was their agent. Cyn continued typing as he spoke. "Mykle... Yup, we have it. Al just called and we forced it through... No, the numbers didn't work. It doesn't matter... I'm authorized to approve a hundred and fifty grand... it'll go... ciao."

The following day was the last day of the eight-nine offering. It was going to be a busy day and according to plan the MOB moved branch operations to Kaleidoscope on Façade. They set up a production line with all hands on deck on site for 'Off-site Loans Closings'.

Technical support checked the connection to CCAP as retail bankers sat beside investment bankers handling a step transaction that had to be fully coordinated to be documented and signed by midnight.

The MOB had to process a 'Daylight Loan' for some two hundred investors to set up each with personal loans, transfer funds and close two hundred matching non-bank notes in one business day.

It required teamwork and they would get more people if they had to.

Bræn, Cyn and Sully worked side by side with the assistance of bank staff loaned from the branch. They opened files and handed tax savers' documents to brokers that manufactured debt in taxpayers' names.

Robby's file landed on Bræn's desk and he recognized it as one of the more difficult. He checked Al's handwritten amount and figures and decided he would date it, but he passed it on for Cyn to key it in.

Bræn took his pen and dated the note December 1st, and wrote '89' on the line for the year. He bundled the documents and passed them to Cyn as he started another package. "This is one of yours," he said.

Cyn took with a sigh. He didn't care who did which investor. He was completely focused on the job in hand with no time to think of any nuances in completion. Cyn couldn't distinguish it from any other to remember even as he checked the amount on the bank-demand note, although he wondered why it was dated already. He had just a few minutes to do his part in MOB and Kaleidoscope loans closings.

Cyn reviewed the 'Terms and Conditions' screen with CCAP data entry lines and completion codes from adjudication. He checked the client profile screen for Mr and Mrs Ducky and tabbed the cursor to the property search line. He typed a code for 'No Encumbrances' and pressed a function key to access the 'New Account Setup' screen that transposed data including the new client's name and address.

The account codes checked with the product code AKLP 89 and Cyn looked at the note before keying 100,000.00 and 12/300 terms at 1% over prime at 14.5% in 1,370.00 monthly payments. His data entry changed the file status code to 'COMPLETED' and he pressed a key to end a transaction that advanced funds for a loan-dependent sale.

The date and time was on the screen and in the log the clock ticked through one sixtieth – on par for a one-second 'Daylight' loan.

The last screen was the 'Closing Screen' and all that remained was to type a destination code for the account of Mykle's law firm, Ardent Bailiffs, and press the Enter key to release the funds.

There, it was done... Robby's credit was gone. Another one... Good.

Cyn looked at the loan application checklist and ticked the last item, 'Confirmation Sent' that advised the dealer. Not the debtor, there was never any intention of doing anything to give the game away.

At the end of each loan transaction, the clerk behind the bank officer that opened the file took it back with a special duty to double check each bank-demand note was filled out and dated and signed with an Affidavit of Subscribing Witness to identify the recipient by name.

On the strict condition sworn witness to signatures matched those on bank-demand notes; bankers removed cardboard document corners to separate and review signed documents. Bank loan forms that passed inspection had to be detached from investment contracts because each investor's note had to be priced accordingly and properly signed in witness whereof to eventually, and in total, close the entire deal.

The clerk inserted bank documents in a folder secured with an elastic strap in the flap. Bank originals were put in boxes on one side and investment contract originals moved to eager brokers on the other.

Dealers wrote quantities and prices on subscription agreements and loan amounts on investors' notes. Mykle L'Æmori signed non-bank note IOUs in witness and acceptance as real money thereof.

After months of preparation the MOB finagled several hundred loans to advance some ten million loonies to Kaleidoscope reselling their own mortgage on their own head office on Façade as an investment that valued property at twice the cost in future tax credits.

The last eighty-nine 'Off-site Loans Closings' transaction took place in Kaleidoscope's office on Façade around six that evening. It raised a cheer from steely-eyed bankers.

All eyes turned to Mykle L'Æmori in the final act of signing the last investor's note in acceptance of money thereof. He signed it and put his pen down and stood up to look around the room. He linked his fingers and straightened his arms with a twist to push his sticky palms outwards with hands locked to crack stiff joints for quick relief.

It was quiet enough for people to hear him crack. He rolled his hands inwards and rubbed them together as he often did when he thought of money. His face broke into a smile as a sure sign of job satisfaction. He grinned as the team smiled with him and they let out another cheer.

Kaleidoscope people stood up to face the bankers who made it possible. They were surrounded by boxes full of documents that some would go to the MOB leaving the rest with Kaleidoscope. They smiled and shook hands and everybody thanked everyone for a job well done. "Well done," Cyn said shaking sticky hands.

It had been a long day and Mykle rewarded the team with pizzas delivered for a party with wine and drinks for everybody's taste. They filled plastic tumblers some-times raised with hollers and cheers as they drank and relaxed in blessed relief... the graft was over.

All that remained for Cyn was to put MOB bank-demand notes in a safe. It was his job to see it through to the end. He called dispatch for a security van with instructions who to find, and what to pick up.

Cyn left the group and followed the truck to see the step transaction into the bank. The all-important document boxes were stacked on a dolly made to measure. Each bank box had hand written names and account numbers on labels above shiny grommet fingerholes in the dark sides of filed cases that made a wavy pattern in their numbers.

The van arrived at the Osowega branch and Cyn got out to unlock the backdoor to enter the bank. He pressed the code and went in to open the vault. He and security cameras watched as men pushed the boxes inside on a dolly they left under an over-hanging sign:

LOG ASSETS AND STORE IN ALPHABETICAL ORDER.

The driver checked the load and Cyn signed the shipping docket the guard signed and to leave a copy for the bank and one for dispatch.

Cyn's hand lingered to stroke the boxes fondly. He patted the material for everything the MOB would ever need if it came to an argument with investors. God forbid a class action.

He thought of bonuses all round and turned to leave. He shut the vault door and listened to the reassuring clanking noises of bolts closing as he walked after the couriers to see them on their way.

The box with Robby's name on it represented three hundred thousand loonies in present and ten-year cash flow from double-digit interest tax credits claimed as cost of savings for the government to pay.

He was one of countless 'Sitting Ducks' with no idea what next.

Making Sense Fake Money

The day after the eighty-nine closings started as any other bank day for Cyn except for calm after the business rush. All the manual work to generate cash flow was done. Interest accumulated automatically at the stroke of midnight from the previous day's 'Daylight' loans.

Cyn relaxed. He could report the default swap to Phil Morrsacs and expect his Christmas bonus for doing God's work. He knew he would be lauded as a hero and praised for his innovative lending methods.

Profit travels fast in computer systems and the moment he saw his computer screen he was overjoyed to see his name as a new addition to those rewarded with trips to St Lucia for exceeding quota. He could see his name and Executive Loans Manager title with his Bræn Chyld and Sully VanScrawl as joint winners from the Osowega branch. What an honor. He leaned back in his high chair dreaming of the commendations that would surely come with the invitation.

A week passed in gloating before Cyn Fordo settled down to collect revenue from Kaleidoscope tax credits. All that remained was sending belated terms and conditions and requests for payments for bank loans that still failed to advise Robby Ducky he had a tax credit savings loan account number in MOB 'Off-the-balance' sheet bookkeeping.

It was the same for Mykle L'Æmori basking in the glory of a scheme under way to pay his mortgage from tax credits taken in advance of being claimed by thrifty people that worked hard to get them.

He had reason to be very pleased with himself. He was instantly five million loonies better off having sold his property to investors that borrowed ten million to payout a five million demand note on it.

Mykle sat back in his office chair and contemplated his future cash flow from papered non-bank notes that he could resell as CDO – Collateralized Debt Obligations – in financial markets, and still collect from investors in default. He thought of the high cost of the Badio Dinwuddy audit report to fool investors. Never mind, it was in the purchase price. For now he had to wait for the MOB to send remittance letters to investors that would start bank revenue streams before he could launder non-bank notes for cash through taxation systems.

The final stage of making sense fake money was a letter from a bank previously unknown to investors asking for money without letting on it was a personal loan rather than a mortgage. For people ready to save tax credits in a mortgage to buy property the con was as simple as bank jargon alluding to investment financing in the first and only correspondence from the MOB about a Kaleidoscope 'Unit'.

Since there was only one account for all investors' payments, Cyn had to compose a remittance letter requesting twelve postdated cheques in separate bookkeeping records geared to keep people in the dark and rating agencies and out of the loop. Millions of investors like Ducky fell into a personal debt trap disguised as a mortgage.

December 14, 1989

Dear Mr. Ducky

As you know MOB provided equity financing for your recent Kaleidoscope 89 Limited Partnership unit purchase and we are pleased to confirm the details of your investment loan.

LOAN TYPE/NUMBER: Personal Demand Loan, Term Basis
AMOUNT: 110,354.00
INTEREST RATE: Prime + 1%
REPAYMENT TERMS: 1370.78 per month on a 25 year amortization
METHOD OF PAYMENT: 12 post dated cheques

Your loan has been set up for a term of twelve months with payments commencing January 2, 1990. In this regard, we would appreciate you forwarding us a series of 12 post dated cheques in the amount of 1370.78.

While your loan payment amount was set up for a twelve month period, prime rate may fluctuate from time to time which would necessitate adjustments to payments. This should only occur if there are dramatic increases to the prime rate. Should this happen we would certainly provide you with reasonable notice.

At the end of the first twelve month term and annually thereafter, we will be in contact with you to conduct a renewal review. If you have any questions in the meantime, please contact the undersigned. Thank you for allowing us to be of service to you.

Yours truly,

Executive Loans Manager

Cyn was proud of his letter. MOB legal checked it for providing information and transferring responsibility to recipient debtors that had to deny previous knowledge to stop the fraud. Otherwise it was deemed they knew about equity financing with an investment loan and a personal demand loan in the letter. They paid not knowing it was a personal loan filled out by the bank on their behalf for one unit of Kaleidoscope described for the purpose of buying property.

There was no contact number for Cyn Fordo and only one investor in three hundred called him for clarification. Most everyone spoke to financial advisors involved in making debt as the wrong people to ask to explain it. "It's a tax sheltered mortgage, you pay the bank to claim it back as an expense paid for by the government," Al said.

For years people told courts they thought they had a mortgage. But the testimony was trashed by judges handing out summary judgments to banks collecting personal loans tied to tax shelter sales.

In the Appeal Court the case of Robby Ducky was judged by Madam Justice Lu'Squeeze flanked by McFulland and L'Flume that found no fault with loan documentation for trial with respect to the MOB. In the Court's opinion Robby could not have misunderstood the role of the bank. Mdm Justice referred to the bank's lending technology and told the accused, *"You could not have not known you had a loan."*

Kaleidoscope deals were sold far and wide to a varied group of people. Some knew what they were doing, and indeed some were rich enough, or just too busy to do anything. But most were sitting ducks like Robby. They had no idea it was a game for the MOB to sell loans for Kaleidoscope selling a mortgage to flip their own property, and for financial advisors to profit from putting people into debt – in Al's case, his own wife, not to mention the government.

Many were taken in; lawyers, politicians and even bankers plunged into debt. Only a plumber plugged the leak in his own case. It wasn't understanding that caused him to call the MOB to ask to speak to Cyn Fordo, it was just by chance they spoke to each other.

"Yes, he's at the Osowega branch, I'll connect you."

The call went straight through. "Cyn Fordo speaking."

"I 'ave a letter about ta mortgage payments." Mr Plumber spoke from an office phone with the speaker on for his wife to hear.

Cyn was surprised. A workman's brogue put him off guard. "What?"

"It's t'mortgage in't ya letter."

Cyn had millions of loonies in mortgages in the branch and he wondered why this client call came through to him. He went back to basic customer training. He tabbed through a menu to an inquiry screen, "Yes sir… right, what's your account number?"

The caller didn't bank with the MOB so he looked at the letter to find a number. He couldn't find one. "Hold t'on t'missus might know."

It was Cyn's error that he didn't catch on to what the call was about.

"Nope, there's no number 'ere."

"You have a letter from me?" Cyn scrolled to identify the caller, then it dawned. "It's about Kaleidoscope?"

"Yup."

Having started badly Cyn made it more confusing with jargon. "It's equity financing for a tax shelter," he said.

"That's t'same as mortgage?"

"No, well in this case, yes." Cyn didn't want to explain derivatives to a neophyte. But as the conversation went, he didn't have to.

"This is Mrs Plumber," another voice piped in. "We don't bank with you. We'd rather not. Could we send our savings to Kaleidoscope?"

"That wouldn't work." Cyn became and sounded cagy.

"Oh, it's alright, we usually pay cash for everything," she said.

"That's 'ow we 'andle t'money," Mr Plumber agreed. "We'll get on t'blower an' talk to sales rep, thank'ee. G'bye."

Cyn had no chance to reel them in. "Hm, good bye," he said.

Cyn knew what he had to do. In this game duds had to be eaten by reps that sold them, to sell them on. He pressed a dial button to reach Mykle. It rang and promptly switched to an answering machine.

Cyn spoke after the tone: "Hi Mykle, this is Cyn calling. We have a dud with a Mr Plumber. You'd better call the rep that sold it to take it back. Let me know who it is and we'll swap names. Okay?"

Cyn had some loose ends to clear up. Audit was still questioning Mr Ducky's credit capabilities. He decided he had to a stop to any more collateral deficiency notifications.

TO/DESTINATION: LISIA
FROM: CYN FORDO
DATE: DEC 14, 1989
SUBJECT: ROBBY DUCKY
THE LIEN THAT REFLECTS 100 M HAS BEEN CONFIRMED BY MANAGER AT T/D TO BE PAID DOWN TO 4800 & IS PART OF HTX TO CCAB – ATTACHED NO FURTHER REPORTING REQ'D.

Cyn had just finished typing the message into CCAP when Mykle returned his call. He picked up the phone.

"Cyn?"

"Mykle…" He was relieved to talk. "Did you get my message?"

"Mm. We found the rep. It's Trixie Clawback. She knows about it and will take it until she sells it on. She'll sign up as the investor."

"That's alright then."

"So it looks good, mmm?" Mykle wanted to know when to send his letter that welcomed investors to Kaleidoscope. "We have to deliver records of the deal before Christmas."

Cyn confirmed he was satisfied bank funding was secure. "Other than the one that got away, they're all hooked and cooked."

In concert with Cyn's 'As you know' letter, Mykle was just as clever writing a letter of thanks that expressed his pleasure and good wishes for Christmas and a decade of peace he wanted until default. It was perfectly composed to deliver a ten-year plan to defraud.

December 18, 1989

Dear Mr. Ducky,

We are pleased to confirm the offering by Kaleidoscope Limited Partnership (89) of 166 limited partnership interests closed on December 1, 1989, and that your subscription of two limited partnerships was accepted on that date.

We want to take this opportunity to thank you for investing in Kaleidoscope Limited Partnership (89). Every effort has been made, and will be made, to ensure that the investment lives up to your expectations.

The record book relating to your investment is enclosed. It consists of your personal investment summary, a copy of the limited partnership agreement, a copy of your subscription agreement, a copy of your investor note, and a certificate evidencing your limited partnership interests. We will provide you with the material necessary to file your tax return, including audited financial statements, by the end of March next year.

As you know Kaleidoscope Limited Partnership (89) will make cash distri-butions following the end of each calendar quarter. Accordingly, you can expect your first distribution cheque in January of next year.

We will make every effort to keep you appraised as to the status of your investment. If you have any questions in the meantime, please do not hesitate to contact our office.

Finally, we ask that ask you assist our communication efforts by advising us to any change of address or errors in the address we are currently using.

As the holiday season in now in full swing and a new and promising decade is almost upon us, we want to take this opportunity to wish you a happy holiday and a happy and peaceful new decade.

Yours very truly,

Kaleidoscope Limited Partnership (89)

On behalf of the General Partner, ▮9933 Ogstowne Ltd.

Kaleidoscope sent investment record books out in time for Christmas. Al delivered Robby's with a greetings card and congratulations for becoming an owner of tax sheltered property on Façade.

Kaleidoscope Limited Partnership (89)
Mr. Robby Ducky
PERSONAL INVESTMENT SUMMARY

Date Closed: December 1, 1989 # of Interests: 2

Property Location:	41-43-45 Façade, Ogstowne, Hontaria
Amount Invested:	110,354.94 Equity
	61,647.06 Investor Note
	172,000.00 Total Investment

FINANCING

Branch:	MOB, Osowega Contact: Cyn Fordo
Terms of Loan:	Prime + 1% floating to be reviewed annually for the next ten years. Blended principal and interest payments based on a 25 year amortization.

PARTNERSHIP HIGHLIGHTS

General Partner:	9933 Ogstowne Ltd.
	P.O. Box 13 Queen Key West
Contact:	Daveh Gumn or Mykle L'Æmori
Cash Distributions:	100% of Distributable Cash at the end of each calendar quarter before January 1, 2000, will be distributed to the Limited Partners in accordance with their respective Pro-Rata Shares. Distributable Cash will be distributed at the end of each calendar quarter thereafter as follows: 25% to the General Partner and 75% to the Limited Partners in accordance with their respective Pro-Rata's.
Liquidity:	On a periodic basis the General Partner will have the Property Appraised and will formulate a recommend-ation respecting disposition or retention of the Property. The recommendation will be put before the Limited Partners at a meeting duly called for that purpose. The Limited Partners will have the opportunity to accept, modify or reject recommendation by Special Resolution which by definition requires approval by at least two-thirds of the votes cast at a duly constituted meeting.

A belated loan 'Term and Conditions' letter that appeared to refer to a mortgage from the MOB, and a fait accompli investment record sans mortgage from Kaleidoscope sealed the fate of Robby Ducky and tens of tens of thousands like him taken for a ride in the Great Divide.

Thrifty people's savings paid by cheque to the MOB poured in for income tax credit receipts printed a year later and each year thereafter for ten years. Kaleidoscope did the same, but they took cash from rent to pay mortgage interest for ten years due to rent consignments never revealed by anyone, including the tax shelter auditor Badio Dinwuddy.

Al Fudgit combined MOB loan and Kaleidoscope mortgage interest charges in so-called 'Mortgage Partnership' claims by which Robby helped the government lose money by tax avoidance and evasion.

Robby wasn't the only investor claiming interest on tax-worthinesses for the likes of L'Æmori collecting mortgage derivative interest laundered for cash through taxation systems. Bank-loan-dependent ABCP Third Party Notes in circulation generated revenue streams from CDO – Collateralized Debt Obligations from investments sold by MOB agent such as Kaleidoscope Equities Corporation.

When ABCP financial conduits seized in August 2008 making banks insolvent, the Prime Compounder bailed out some thirty-two billion non-bank notes in a 'Montroyal Accord' that gave immunity to banks from prosecution in what was called the Confoundation solution.

Robby read the bank's memorandum about funding Kaleidoscope limited partnerships. It announced the bank's objective addressed to a long list of managers that described Kaleidoscope as a MOB project, 'To acquire and own an income-producing retail store and office/commercial building at 41-43-45 Façade.'

It was a front, a commercial game of Monopoly for bigger players than Robby Ducky as a pawn rather than a customer. In the years that followed, Kaleidoscope incorporated some thirteen properties for elite tenants, even bankers underwriting mortgages sold as investments.

The tax shelter produced losses as promised until the partners voted to sell property they thought they owned back to Kaleidoscope as the fifty-one percent majority shareholder taking possession.

After mortgage default, dumping a losing proposition made fools of investors. Mykle L'Æmori reacquired his own head office building in a rollover deal he embraced as his thirteenth acquisition to add to a REIT the bank engaged him to manage in MOB Capital Markets.

Robby reported the flip as a non-arm's-length deal to the Conjurer the same as Gofa had done for duped investors. But they dropped it without hesitation for lack of evidence of any criminal wrongdoing. The Secret Claw Society ruled the same; they said L'Æmori was entitled to take as many oaths as he wanted for as many loans as the MOB could handle. Every agency said sinful was lawful in the Great Divide.

In an extraordinary turn of events over ten years, Robby wrote his experience as a target, *The Perfect Sting,* with a letter of introduction from the MOB claiming all their demand notes are clearly marked with the bank's logo. It became an important reference to make a case to regulate banks and curb irresponsible lending. It started Petition 44 in Hontaria with party leaders speaking out for consumer safeguards to protect people from losing their life savings and their homes to wayward lenders involved in sleazy storybook tax shelter schemes.

It was retribution for Robby Ducky, made a debtor by a system.

To this day 'Sitting Duck' loans remain legal for an easy rip-off with no risk to banks that sell loans in the small print of tax shelter schemes. Al got Bobbie to sign a note and Kaleidoscope resubmitted a previous used eighty-nine 'Statements of Affairs' for another loan. It was so cool. The MOB commingled it with the first for another unsigned, undisclosed, undocumented tied loan to close another sale.

Again Robby and Bobbie weren't the only ones. As long as agents for the bank notarized bank-paid witness to people's signatures for loan-dependent non-bank notes paid by a government that was willing to pay tax credits for ABCP claims, they were happy making money.

Robby likened lenders to cuckoo birds that deposit eggs in nests of a different kind. Lying for a hatchling to cull the clutch and devour food until maturity. Similarly deceived, Robby fed Kaleidoscope's mortgage until it became a fully fledged financial nightmare with liability hedged to a credit default swap *and* personal indebtedness to a bank waiting to collect its note in a trick tax credit savings loan account.

Robby Ducky did his best to demonstrate revenue streams from toxic loans to lawyers and judges and politicians that seemed blind to any wrongdoing to stop non-bank notes monetizing false tax credit claims.

He felt had to explain the rules of the game to the Queen printed on her money in his pocket, what else could he do?

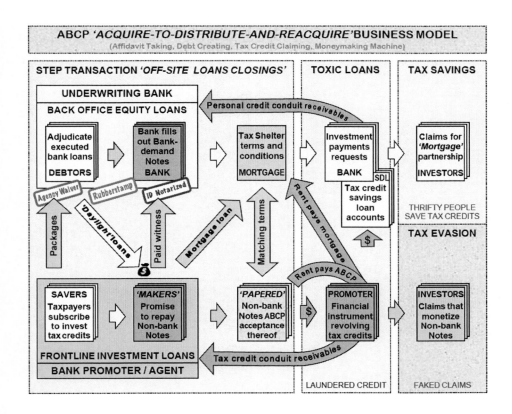

ABCP 'ACQUIRE-TO-DISTRIBUTE-AND-REACQUIRE' BUSINESS MODEL
(Affidavit Taking, Debt Creating, Tax Credit Claiming, Moneymaking Machine)

| STEP TRANSACTION 'OFF-SITE LOANS CLOSINGS' | TOXIC LOANS | TAX SAVINGS |

UNDERWRITING BANK
BACK OFFICE EQUITY LOANS
Personal credit conduit receivables

| Adjudicate executed bank loans — DEBTORS | Bank fills out Bank-demand Notes — BANK | Tax Shelter terms and conditions — MORTGAGE | Investment payments requests — BANK SDL | Claims for 'Mortgage' partnership — INVESTORS |

Tax credit savings loan accounts

THRIFTY PEOPLE SAVE TAX CREDITS

Agency Waiver · Rubberstamp · ID Notarized
Packages · Daylight loans · Paid witness · Mortgage loan · Matching terms · Rent pays mortgage · Rent pays ABCP

TAX EVASION

| SAVERS — Taxpayers subscribe to invest tax credits | 'MAKERS' — Promise to repay Non-bank Notes | 'PAPERED' — Non-bank Notes ABCP acceptance thereof | PROMOTER — Financial instrument revolving tax credits | INVESTORS — Claims that monetize Non-bank Notes |

FRONTLINE INVESTMENT LOANS
BANK PROMOTER / AGENT
Tax credit conduit receivables

LAUNDERED CREDIT · FAKED CLAIMS

Over the years, investors like Robby Ducky paid the MOB for loans they thought were mortgages to own income-producing real estate. L'Æmori collected and reported mortgage-derived interest that diverted income tax from the Queen of Torts. Finally, in default, the general failure of ABCP financial conduits triggered a global credit crunch. The Confoundation Gallows Prosecutor found tax savers guilty of making non-bank notes and ruled all banks immune from prosecution.

L'Æmori did nothing wrong in the eyes of the law. He made a fortune for bankers that praised him as St Mykle of Lucre. The Prime Compounder made an order that taxpayers buy back non-bank notes in circulation.

It wasn't the Queen's money. Counterfeit! What else could they do?

Capitalism without Capital

The MOB took pleasure from the Appeal Court ruling and prepared a detailed *'Examination for Execution'* to collect. Ozegle sat down with a huge binder of documents about Robby's finances including a last minute fax wired to the court recorder from Gofa Beres.

Ozegle listed a dozen undertakings from examination. He wanted five year's bank records released to the MOB and seven year's history of all credit card transactions. Ozegle ordered release of tax records from Gofa and a record of college fees paid through the years. The MOB said it was entitled to claw back any money they deemed to be gifted.

Robby had no choice but to pay the bank. He couldn't bear the idea of a MOB chasing his children to repossess money he paid for university fees. He got his lawyer to make a deal to settle for eighty thousand.

The bank approved the amount but Ozegle said his legal costs award was fixed. Robby wrote a cheque to the bank with the balance in cash to satisfy its debt collector. He took it to the bank's law firm where it was counted in the presence of an independent witness and he left with a signed receipt and acknowledgement to clear paid writs.

It could and should have ended the story. Robby was ready to give up the lawsuit the MOB told the court it wasn't litigating. But Ozegle was hungry and carried on litigating with an email to Robby's lawyer, Wire Tedd. They claimed they were short-changed a thousand loonies.

When Robby heard about it he realized how risky it was paying cash to lawyers. He was somewhat relieved to have only lost a thousand. It was malicious and it hurt, but they could have screwed much more.

It wasn't a money issue. The MOB wanted release from prosecution for its agents. Calls that had once been between lawyers changed to harassment that Robby recorded on his phone.

The bank's lawyer sounded angry in a composed sort of way that comes with practice and courtroom experience. It was about his cost award from Justice Renta-Horse. "There's two issues," he said. "First we can't take cash. And second, we're missing a thousand loonies."

The lawyer was clear he wanted Robby to come back to his office with more money.

"I paid you all the money you wanted."

"You shortchanged us. Are you saying that girl at the desk took it?"

"I'm not saying."

"You have to make up the difference."

That evening Robby and Bobbie decided to go to the bank with a draft rather than handing cash to its shifty lawyer. It amused him to see a banker's draft made out to the President of the MOB signed by the President. He delivered it in person to the Head Office on Buy Street.

Robby and Bobbie hoped it would close the affair given they had a receipt from the bank's agent to remove paid writs.

A parcel he was expecting arrived by courier and Robby remembered the last time he did what he was thinking of to promote his book. It was his famous duck costume. He was keen to see it as he broke through plastic wrapping to open the box. He looked at the soft yellow velvet fabric cut in layered fringes. "Hello my friend," he said.

Robby lifted it out and it spread into the shape of a duck. He thought out loud as he held it up in front of him. "Perfect."

The costume was designed to be convincing. It was a duck complete with yellow feathers, wings, legs, and a goofy head with a broad beak. He took it to the bedroom and stepped into an obvious opening in the bodice to climb into. He looked in the closet mirror and smiled.

The gear had a wire and metal frame and he giggled as he fiddled with the belt-buckle he remembered not to jump when it clicked into shape. The body swelled out with a bulge in the back for a tail. He removed his glasses and picked up his headgear that except for the beak, eyes and feathered topknot looked like a balaclava. He stretched it over his head and connected Velcro fasteners round the neck. Then he wriggled his arms through loopholes to attach floppy wings to his elbows with his hands holding the ends in loose-fitting cloves.

It was really good. Robby bobbed and flapped his wings for a bird effect in the mirror. It was a funny outfit and his legs in blue jeans made it look ridiculous. He smiled, thinking he should have dressed in yellow tights and cloth webbed feet first to cover his legs and shoes.

Robby was thinking about 'Sitting Duck' loans when it occurred to him he still had to write fiction the same as a 'truth-of-the-court' transcript that in his case read like comic relief. He knew couldn't name people in such a fantastic story. The court ruled no credible evidence for trial. Wire Tedd warned Robby the MOB and its agents had cause to sue him for making false accusations.

It was a tale and he wanted to make a statement when he launched his latest volume. It was a matter of redemption. But as he looked at the stupid big yellow bird with blue legs… he began to get cold feet.

The phone rang.

The duck turned quickly and stepped out of the mirror. Robby was hampered with metalwork round his calves. It made him step with an awkward gate. He waddled as he slowed down to reach the phone. The yellow bird bobbed and swayed as it came to a halt. The costume designer would be pleased to know it had that effect.

It was a struggle for Robby to stand and he lashed out his wings to keep his balance. He couldn't help his arms lunging forward to grab the sides of the table to stop him keeling over. He stood crouched over the phone with his beak touching the table and his tail in the air. Robby paused for breath. The phone was in front of him and with no thought for himself; he tried to read the numbers on the call display.

The phone rang as he squinted but he knew he couldn't read a thing without his glasses. It was impossible anyway with a veil in the hood that hid human eyes behind painted black dots in white crescents.

He could make out the speaker button and he pressed it to hear the caller on the phone. It was the bank's overenthusiastic lawyer Robby apparently called '*my friend*' in the summary judgment transcript.

Robby tried to lift his head off to talk. He pulled it one way and then the other. The lawyer speaking had no idea there was a commotion.

If the Gallows Prosecutor wanted Robby's head it wouldn't separate with Velcro that stuck like feathers to a sheet. Robby heard plastic tearing sounds, but he couldn't hear the lawyer… and he was deaf to his own heavy breathing as he became exhausted in the struggle.

Robby gave up trying to get his ears out to listen. He tried to hear through padding and velvet that covered his head. He spoke as best he could, and the lawyer assumed the distortion was a poor line.

The MOB's lawyer had written they would continue suing Robby Ducky he confirmed in his call about the problem he had with real money. "We can't take large amounts of cash, we want you to take it back and give us a cheque, or a banker's draft. We can meet you at a bank and we'll give you one of our cheques."

"You've been paid." Robby had read the lawyer's letters and he was concerned and upset. "You're threatening to sue me all over again. You don't make idle threats. You terrify me." He raised his voice. "I've given you money, what's wrong with money?"

Mr Ozegle struggled with his money problem as much as Robby did keeping his head. "I'm really not threatening you sir. Look, your wife can come and sign a cheque if you feel uncomfortable."

Robby was more than uncomfortable. It was like a furnace in his silly costume. He was hot and sticky and sweat was running down his neck to his collar that became soaking wet.

The lawyer was short of money and he was short of breath. "I can't breathe," Robby gasped. "I can't breathe…"

The debt maker/collector was oblivious to any stress caused while he came round to his reason for calling. "The bank will sign a mutual release."

Robby found the energy to speak from anger within, "I don't want a release. I don't want anything from the bank. I just want it to stop."

The line went quiet and Robby was frustrated and confused.

"I don't understand anything in this. It never ends. How is it possible you got all the evidence thrown out of court? I don't understand it."

The lawyer had been on the phone about twenty minutes. Even he had had enough. "You lost, Mr Ducky, I will talk to the bank and we will see if they want you to sign a release. OK? Goodbye."

Robby lifted the handset and let it drop in its cradle to disconnect.

He returned to the bedroom to remove his sweaty garb. He freed his head and looked at a greenish sickly face over a fat yellow belly on blue legs reflected in the mirror. It was an appalling picture. Robby looked at it out of focus and he realized the depth of his despair.

He stood staring in the mirror until he was calm enough to decide how to get his bill down off a duck. He stepped out and dropped the charade on the floor and stepped aside. He was ready to sit and he rested on a stool at Bobbie's dressing table the other side of the room.

It was ten years ago the MOB said he had to pay a debt because he was a sitting duck. He objected to being named after a loan, but that is what he saw in the mirror. He said, "SD for '*Sitting Duck*'".

Robby rested his head in his hands and looked in the oval dressing table mirror angled towards the closet mirror behind him. It was like a big kaleidoscope. He could see himself front and back in continuous multiple reflections from where he sat including a distant view of Ogstowne with bank towers on Buy Street through a looking glass.

It looked as though he was coming and going, front and back, in a weird world of finance. It was then he saw through the scheme.

Robby spoke to the mirror image. "Money lies in Wonderland."

Buy Street isn't one-way. It has credits and debits coming and going.

"Sitting duck loans one way, sovereign debt the other," Robby said.

He thought of Al Fudgit. "Where do homeless accountants live?" he raised his hand in the mirror to answer. "Tax shelters," he chortled.

Al had his own wife Cory sign a promissory note to make a sale for a referral fee. Maybe the MOB dropped a lawsuit to collect because he would have testified that L'Æmori was the agent for the bank.

Robby thought he knew why the MOB lied in court to avoid a trial. Apart from Al setting Bobbie up with an undocumented loan to sell another investment to Robby… the bank didn't want it known the scheme was geared to rob the Queen of Confoundation.

Robby took a banknote from his pocket and wrote on it to define the SD2SD business model. He sang "In Praise of Notes in Red" as he wondered, "Does the Queen pay sovereign debt?"

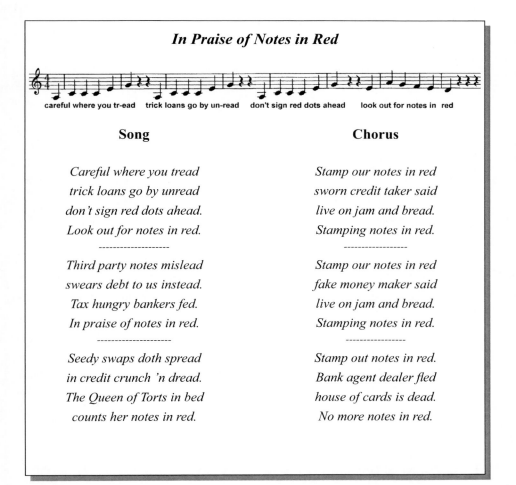

In Praise of Notes in Red

careful where you tr-ead   trick loans go by un-read   don't sign red dots ahead   look out for notes in red

Song	Chorus
Careful where you tread	Stamp our notes in red
trick loans go by unread	sworn credit taker said
don't sign red dots ahead.	live on jam and bread.
Look out for notes in red.	Stamping notes in red.
--------------------	------------------
Third party notes mislead	Stamp our notes in red
swears debt to us instead.	fake money maker said
Tax hungry bankers fed.	live on jam and bread.
In praise of notes in red.	Stamping notes in red.
---------------------	-----------------
Seedy swaps doth spread	Stamp out notes in red.
in credit crunch 'n dread.	Bank agent dealer fled
The Queen of Torts in bed	house of cards is dead.
counts her notes in red.	No more notes in red.

Bobbie was called from work to visit Robby in hospital. He lay on a gurney with an oxygen tube and wires attached to monitor his heart after an ischemic attack he couldn't remember happening.

Bobbie blamed her husband's breakdown on threatening phone calls and letters the MOB would continue to sue for more money. He had the attack when they found the bank hadn't cleared paid writs so they couldn't sell their house to fly away. Ozegle wrote he would sue Robby unless she signed a release for the MOB and its agents to quit her claim they stole her identity for a trick loan to sell a tax shelter.

Despite the insanity that changed their lives, and not daring to speak in fear of being overheard, the couple were still together on what they had to do. Robby wanted to write to explain himself to his Queen.

Bobbie had lived systems with her husband some twenty years. She had documented hundreds of JAD business models for him and was just as skilled in business analysis, but not in group dynamics to lead a workshop. She left the hospital with a banknote Robby secretly pressed into her hand when they kissed farewell. He whispered, "I would like to apologize to the Queen for my part in sovereign debt."

He had written a cryptic note as he did running a JAD: 'Does' above a picture of a youthful Queen and underlined 'pay' in 'I promise to pay the bearer on demand the sum of...' line that he finished 'SD2SD'.

Bobbie understood why Robby wanted to write his Queen, but she wasn't sure it would do any good. This was the Confoundation. They lived in Wonderland. There was a picture of the Queen watching over the bench when a judge chastised Robby and threw out the evidence. Also when a judge accepted a Factum handed over by the MOB to replace the one Robby filed in court. Another picture of the Queen witnessed the bank denying litigating the second note to avoid trial.

Bobbie thought, "Who's to say the Queen isn't a card in the game?"

A doctor released Robby and advised Bobbie to help him relax. Wire Tedd saw Robby the same day with the same advice. He told them to give up their claims against the bank for the sake of their health.

"You can see what happens. Judges say these loans are legal. No one will ever allow your case in court in Confoundland. It's time to quit."

It wasn't the advice Robby wanted to hear from a lawyer who was seemed just as determined to obstruct justice as Oink and Co. Robby briefed Wire Tedd to argue tax issues in the appeal. He wanted Wire to litigate the counterclaim. He wanted to answer a lengthy Motion for Particulars and file the evidence before the court. And he wanted to sue their previous lawyer. But Wire did none of it.

Robby's new lawyer didn't seem to do anything except bill to quit. He told them the evidence would never be allowed in court.

"I'm here to protect you," Wire said. "You will need all the parties to sign mutual releases or else they will sue you for years to come."

Wire drafted a proposal the MOB would remove paid writs if Robby quit his counterclaim defense and Bobbie quit her claim. Eventually Wire phoned he had agreement from everyone to quit.

Then he quit.

Once again Robby was without a lawyer. It was not relaxing. He had to represent himself at Avaloan's Motion for Particulars that was just days away. Wire had deleted his response saying it could wait until discoveries. Robby swore an affidavit along with evidence lawyers wanted to deny and persuade a judge the Duckys had no case for trial.

Robby knew it was an exercise in futility from experience. He simply filed the evidence because it was there. He delivered it to Avaloan's lawyer and then to the court to file his own affidavit in person.

Neither Robby nor Bobbie could figure why Wire Tedd quit when he had them ready to give up. They assumed he had betrayed them. Indeed, Avaloan told Robby they would sue him if they didn't go through with a written proposal to discontinue and sign Minutes of Settlement for a court to rule all their claims were null and void.

Wire Tedd delivered a low blow: Avaloan was not Kaleidoscope. Avaloan was an alias for IPC – Investment Planners Club Securities of the same address on Façade that only came to light when it came down to who would sign releases for L'Æmori to escape a lawsuit.

Somehow the law society had circled the wagons round L'Æmori to protect him as agent for the bank for ten years. The final hurdle was litigation the MOB denied to avoid trial that Avaloan, not the bank's agent had to also obfuscate to obstruct justice, or let the writ hit the fan.

In the finality of defeat the Duckys were well and truly plucked. As well as victims of crime they were beaten by heavy-handed lawyers that lay down the law in a paid for roller-coaster ride called jurisprudence.

"I found your duck-suit and returned it," Bobbie told Robby in bed.

"It's okay, I don't need it anymore." He winced. "It was lucky the metal deflected bullets the last time I wore it."

"Lucky." Bobbie glanced at a clock on a television screen that spelled out news in silent tickertape. "It's half past crazy," she teased.

A report showed a younger, then older Queen speaking at the United Relations that make Bobbie think to ask. "Will you write the Queen you were a '*Maker*' of non-bank notes behind her sovereign debt?"

Robby looked at the ceiling with his head in the pillow. "Maybe."

Bobbie watched pictures of fire bombs and people waving banners in city streets. "So Cozy added two years to retirement. There's three million out in protest, fires in the streets, all over the country."

Robby listened as Bobbie spoke of news he didn't care to watch. "A Prime Minister across the pond is having a party. They're celebrating the success of a coalition. They're singing songs and saying nice things about power sharing because it takes two to quango."

Bobbie paused to read the headlines and speak her mind.

"The right complains of labour pains. They say the left left them in debt. The Finance Minister promises to balance the budget. He says they will be firm but fair. They say they can't cut spending on defense so they're going to eliminate child allowances to save a billion. And a flighty Lord wants to cut welfare because it breeds poor people."

Robby chipped in, "Saving a billion in child allowances is a pittance compared to trillions they pay banks. If it wasn't for people saving tax credits there wouldn't be any sovereign debt in non-bank notes."

"The Minister says he has to act now to make sure taxpayers won't have to pay interest-on-interest-on-interest to banks ever again."

Triple interest got Robby's attention. He looked at the newscast and read the reports and started talking about the news the same as Bobbie.

"They have to tighten spending by some hundred and thirteen billion to keep a triple-A credit rating with bankers. They plan to reduce a record deficit of eleven percent of domestic product to two percent in five years. Just listen to the spin." Robby looked at Bobbie. "They say the Confoundation is a world class model of prudent banking."

Confoundation daily papers were not as flattering about the country that broadcast the House Martin's advice to automate government departments as he had done. Bobbie handed a section to Robby to read: 'Austerity Gamble' in one column and 'Welfare State Takes a Pounding' in another.

Bobbie counted numbers in the pounding. "They lose eleven billion a year to tax fraud so they're going to spend a billion to reduce it. I expect that'll be the billion taken from child allowance."

Robby read the article. "They're cutting core programs fifteen percent including what they spend to maintain the Queen's household. The opposition objects to the speed and amount. They say the government is being ideological. Isn't that fantastic? There's no debate about ideology. They've got everyone worked up about child allowances, university fees and adding years to working lives before retirement."

Young and old took to the streets with a common grouse about paying more for less. A student demonstrator putting a boot right through a party head office window became front page news next to statements from world leaders at a G20 far away from home.

"The G20 says there's a currency war and they've launched a trillion QE2 on a tidal wave of debt going round the world." Bobbie kept her husband informed of the highlights. "The Fiddle Reserve can't print money fast enough that costs a bob to press. They've printed a hundred billion in hundreds that won't crease, and it may have to be destroyed."

Robby read the bottom line. "It cost taxpayers a hundred million for worthless paper." He laughed, but he didn't think it was funny.

Toxic loan lawsuits landed everywhere.

A local global bank being sued for nine billion for taking kickbacks in schemes that made off with sixty-five billion took up the front page. It was probably a con artist sentenced to jail for one hundred and fifty years for scamming millionaires that made it newsworthy compared to a bank suing the Duckys for ten thousand a year for ten years.

Whereas Al Fudgit's knowledge of trick loans may have stopped the MOB collecting from Mrs Fudgit, Robby discovering the game didn't help in the case of Al setting up a trick loan for Mrs Ducky.

With nine judges deceived and a swapped Factum used to win a court order to collect a hundred thousand loonies, and not cancelling paid writs, Robby sympathized with nations forced to borrow billions to cover sovereign debt. It seemed even a government that complained about potentially criminal bankers in a common market couldn't do anything to challenge the *'I wish debt on taxpayers'*.

Bobbie telegraphed the news. "The banks they nationalized are forced to liquidate public assets selling loans to pay allied liabilities. The government has to cut five billion from social services and increase taxes to ten billion to pay a hundred billion loan at five percent from a fatter figure able to buy money at two percent." She paused for breath and gasped, "I can't keep up with this."

Robby was intrigued with reviews of an *'After the Crash'* history written by former Prime Minister, Hon Gordon Brown who had attended a pre- G20 Wall Street Journal Future of Finance Initiative with Robby Ducky as a participant in March 2009. The Prime Minister had joined delegates in debate at the table next to Robby. He remembered it as a time and place he enjoyed being himself.

Reviewers dissected quotable quotes. "He says the crisis started with subprime mortgages but he blames the banks he had to nationalize and buying a rock that might have been an offshore company." Robby read a City Editor's analysis. "Brown also takes the view that the behaviour [of the banks] was a breach of regulatory rules. *'If there is no criminal law and thus there are no criminal prosecutions to deal with these flagrant abuses, there should be,'* Brown writes."[3]

Bobbie wasn't impressed, "He's a hypocrite. You made your case for banking reforms to *'Strengthen Underwriting Standards'* as the top priority for him to address at his G20 in 2009. He didn't do it. He rewarded his banker friends and he didn't criminalize what they were doing when he knew they were breaking the rules. It's that simple."

Robby agreed, "The *'Kircoddy Donkey'* hasn't got good reviews, but he did sum up what happened in only three words."

"So tell me," Bobbie said wanting to be enlightened.

"Capitalization without capital. That's it in a nutcase."

Bobbie was quick in wonder. "Did he say who capitalized what?"

"No, he blames the deficit on fifty billion bonuses paid to bankers."

"You can't expect him to write shadow banks launder fake Non-bank Notes as capital to make money on bogus claims for tax credits."

"Someone should ask him." Robby said tightly. "It was in my paper."

Bobbie was sympathetic. "He didn't need your paper my darling. He must have known all about it as the Shadow Chancellor. Democ…" Bobbie's stuttered in shock and awe, "…racies vote left or right."

"We vote for shadow governments and shadow banks either way."

"That's why you can't get a fair trial in Confoundation." Bobbie knew her husband couldn't sign a release for the MOB even if it meant them being made homeless. It was his personal moral hazard and she understood his dilemma. "So, are you going write the Queen a judge made you pay a trick loan that papered your note that started the global credit crunch?"

"Haha. That's funny." Knowing the origins of debt hadn't set him free. Not yet. Just his sense of humor. "Trillions speaks for itself. If you want to know how a bank defrauds people saving tax credits, it's quite a simple model." He turned a page, "What do you think?"

"That's better," Bobbie looked at the chart with approval. "It shows how to scam trick mortgages that dump fake loonies in financial markets. If you sent this to the Queen I think she'd understand the origins of sovereign debt, and where her money went."

---

3   Ref: Alex Brummer assesses Gordon Brown's new book. Daily Mail. December 8, 2010

Robby smiled, "It shows how to save loonies in bank loans that pretend to be mortgages that generate invisible earnings in shadow economies. That's why we didn't see the money go until the bank sued us. And, by then it was long gone into a massive money laundering scheme."

"You've told the police about identity theft, toxic loans, tax evasion, money laundering, and a bank holding property ransom to avoid trial, and there's Petition 44 to protect consumers. What more can you do?"

"They won't read Petition 44. The fraud squad never opened a file on my complaint, and they won't accept new evidence. And the police wrote they won't investigate lawyers obstructing justice."

CAPITALISM WITHOUT CAPITAL REVENUE STREAMS
Sitting Duck to Sovereign Debt Business Model

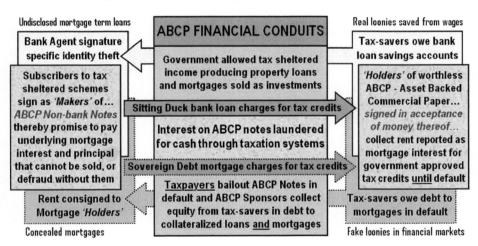

Robby checked the flow. "It's amazing. No one denies I created a non-bank note. They refuse to follow the money, tax credits to the right, cash debits to the left for debt without trial. It's legal. No investigation. No criminal charges. It's the perfect sting with fraud that continues."

Bobbie had had enough of bad news and decided to stop watching after seeing pictures of students swarming a royal carriage waving banners, bashing windows and shouting, "Off with their heads".

The next day papers included pictures of people waving a fond farewell to a favorite flag ship harrier carrier in the Royal Navy.

Robby worried for his Queen having already lost her head on postage stamps as it were, being privatized. "There isn't enough money to keep an Ark Royal Harrier

157

carrier," he said. "All I can do is to advise the Queen how she lost her notes, but will she stop banks making sense fake money? That's what I want to know."

Robby read about bank shares rising to where they had been before. "We should have invested in banks," he said. "They can't fail with taxpayers' bailouts. The sleazier they are at making money the more people buy shares even knowing they're rewarding crime."

He went on. "A universal bank is lending billions of Imperial Minted Fidos to governments that need to grease bankers' arrear zones. They know debt's contaging, but it's all they can do to slow it down, eh?"

"Sounds a bit like the MOB's court order for you to pay their toxic loan with a lien on my house to stop you from borrowing any more money."

That evening the news announced a *'Universal Credit'* to pay people out of work and Robby started to echo the broadcast. "The government says it will make sure it's always worth less to people without a job than earning wages. They say it's needed because honest taxpayers are fed up with perpetual skivers living off the working class."

"We don't need any more news." Bobbie switched the television off as the Prime Minister announced a BSB – Big Society Bank loaded with two hundred million unclaimed deposits to fund a new 'Big Society'. She looked at Robby with a smile. "We know what's next. You know how you learnt how to make fake loonies to save your tax credits in the bank?" Bobbie snuggled close to Robby, "I'm going to show you how to make real loonies when you lose tax credits in the bedroom."

External Vigilance Over Banks

The world changed in the days and weeks that followed. Not just for the Duckys trying to escape judicial persecution and extortion by the MOB, nor tens of thousands of taxpayers demonstrating in the streets of debt laden economies. A wave of discontent spilled over millions of people demonstrating for democracy such as the Duckys as a more attractive alternative to aging autocrats clinging on to power round the globe.

Among bloody revolutions and war in the making, the Chancellor of the Exchequer of the realm resigned over a scandal his bodyguard was closer to his wife than expected with service to protect.

The resignation started a new ball game in politics for past leadership rivals both called Ed. Front page news announced the occurrence as two Ed's better than one to leading from down in street houses ten to eleven.

People were wired and weary of budgetary belt tightening evident in reductions and disappearances of well established institutions. Talk show hosts questioned government policy that libraries had to recruit volunteers to stay open, and schools that couldn't afford to pay lollypop people wrote to parents to see children safely cross the road.

The time Bobbie decided she had had enough of the Confoundation was when angry taxpayers with the most sovereign debt in the Arrears Zone voted to oust hapless politicians that quit after nationalizing failing banks and signing loans to recapitalize unconscionable debt.

In his world of manufactured debt obligations, Robby was traumatized by injustice and obviously biased judges that ruled undisclosed loans legal for banks to make and collect. Replies to his complaints about perjury and interference with a Factum from which a judge ruled no credible evidence for trial were long past due and no longer expected.

The MOB wrote they had signed a Mutual Release waiting for Robby's signature. He was confused enough to countersign it under duress. But it wasn't signed by the bank that had no intention of clearing paid writs unless Bobbie quit a lawsuit alleging identity theft and fraud for a trick loan.

It had been a long and dirty fight with treacherous lawyers out to abuse procedure. Bobbie knew she, like Robby, would never get a fair trial.

They couldn't stop talking about it. "It'll take a judge with the Wisdom of Solomon to sort out this mess," Bobbie said. "The defendants say its past statute of limitations and we've been set up for them to sue us to make us quit."

"It's sickening," Robby brooded. "We've been fleeced by judges that reward lawyers with legal costs when they collude to obstruct justice."

They were quiet for a moment as Bobbie made a decision.

"You'll have to sign what the bank wants to get our house back."

"I'll have to hold my nose," Robby agreed. "The only way for any kind of satisfaction from this is to sue our lawyers."

"They'll blame that frightful man who swapped your Factum."

"Well, there's enough blame to go around. I can't believe the bank went to so much trouble to avoid a trial when we offered to settle and quit so many times. They litigated for ten years and the best they could do was swap my Factum for a judge to find no credible evidence for trial. It's in the transcript…" Robby made a face of disgust. "It's so heinous and beyond belief, you'd think they'd want to settle out of court."

Bobbie wasn't as optimistic. "Closure is not in our story. It'll never go to court. We've seen how lawyers abuse procedure. We know it works. Judges won't hear allegations against banks, especially with proof like ours. We'd just be wasting money on lawyers that'd continue betraying us to protect the bank. It'd be the same dirty game all over again."

Robby thought of the cards in the game. "A ten million commission is a Diamond's best friend." He smiled thinly at the spin about bankers that had to be paid ever increasing bonuses to lend money on Main Street.

"The Queen didn't have to go to court for ten years to question why if the crash was so big her advisors from the School of Economics didn't see it coming." Bobbie stood by her man. "Three Bank Wizards wrote a three page dissertation to apologize to her already."

Robby was quiet as Bobbie continued, "They said you asked a silly question and called you crazy. You have nothing to be sorry for."

"Well…" Robby knew she was right. "We'll have to wait and see if a Joker Merlin beats a King Mervyn for trick loans as usual."

Bobbie agreed. "You send your book to the Queen, how you lost her money, and I'll write the surgeon for ailing economies at the ICB – Independent Commission on Banks. Maybe they'll listen and regulate retail and investment banks separately to protect consumers."

It was doubtful as news of 'Sitting Duck' loans in court and a long overdue call for eternal vigilance over banks took a back page in news of war and destruction. The Confoundation voted with allied forces to make it legal to drop bombs through Arabian nights for a no-fly zone and led the charge to protect freedom fighters shooting it out for democracy. And, another Greek tragedy unfolded with the resignation of Socrates hoding cap in hand for an Arrears Zone loan to recapitalize another structural deficit government pending default.

Toxic Loan Syndromes

Mo Mus spoke from the stage, looking proud and prosperous strutting about with G8 leaders gathered behind him. A microphone attached to a miniature transmitter cast his voice around the massive hall to his troops. He raised his arms, palms upwards and outwards, like an athlete scoring a winning goal. It was sufficient for the conversational hubbub to subside as everyone shifted to look in his general direction.

He didn't wave, or shout, nor did he need a drum roll to attract attention to address his troops that were as relaxed as he was about the glorious victory everyone talked about in reunion. They expected closure from the General to confirm the biggest heist in world history.

"Welcome G8 Contagers," he said with a smile that projected from the screen above the stage. He couldn't have looked more pleased than a pig in truffles. His uniform was cleanly pressed, his hair was trimmed and tinted, and his face was freshly shaven and powder-dry for the camera. He was cool and ready.

His men were smartly dressed in pressed brown trousers and blood-red shirts. Women troopers wore the uniform in pleated skirts and blouses. It seemed appropriate for them to interrupt the General and they let out a cheer to urge him on for what they all wanted to hear.

The general had grown fatter since dispatching G8 on its mission ten years ago. Leading from a desk suited him. He had tubbed out and it looked better for the job. His stomach walked the talk and he said, "You surpassed all our expectations in economic warfare that even as we speak still continues in ever-decreasing circles around the globe.

"Trillions…" He paused to let it sink in. He rubbed his hands in glee. "…Trillions of toxic loans in bad banks and still counting." He stopped pacing to face his protégés and raised his arms. "World bankers are happy, people and governments are in debt beyond their means."

As he spoke his face on the screen behind him blended into a mosaic of flags from round the world. A computerized slide show started an alphabet sequence of nations' names in red letters emblazed in gold. Symbols of sovereignty dissolved into scenes of people marching and rioting in the streets, waving banners about capitalism in the air.

General Mo Mus spoke as national news-bites showed uprisings and destruction. He only had to glance at the screen to sync his diatribe to dramatic scenes that unfolded from flag to flag to flag. It was repetitive, changing only in the extent of force used to quell the riots.

Scenes after a stars-and-stripes flag showed bankers out of work from the collapse of Lemon Broth. Newsworthy enough to raise hackles, but no fisticuffs for a camera's roving eye, just a matter of interest for news reporters to analyze the impacts and business points of view.

The silent newsreel displayed a flag with red and white crosses over blue that merged into headline news announcing the nationalization of the Regal Bank of Scutlend to protect clients' money. The broadcast switched to a reporter in front of a bank's head office talking to an angry protester waving a poster that denounced *Notes in Red* and someone's face dubbed 'Fred the Shred'. Mo Mus started talking.

"Comrades! Contagion is doing God's work. G1 to G7 graduated in rotation to create a new world order. We have no casualties of war. They all returned to these hallowed halls to glorify Mammon the same as you. You are God's eighth company. We have amalgamated twelve more into a G20 Corporation."

Mo Mus looked at his soldiers and they looked back with pride as their leader praised them for what they had done.

The General was a practiced warlord and sleaze monger. This was his eighth tirade timed to images good for campaigns and/or propaganda. It didn't matter what he said or when he raised or lowered his tone. He was rich and powerful and totally corrupt. He simply added spin to a slide show that packed a heavy punch by itself whatever he said.

A credit alert flag, a white cross over blue with blue and white stripes, blurred to people rioting in streets next to historic monuments. They poured into banks, the tellers fleeing or hiding as best they could. A reporter announced cashiers killed amid the ruins.

Next a white flag with pale blue sky above and sea below and golden sun in the middle led to scenes of frantic people in battle with an army fighting against its own citizens protesting foreign banks they blamed for hyperinflation and worthless banknotes.

"You have done your tours of duty. You can retire with pensions and you can keep your spoils of war." The General confirmed what they wanted to hear. "It won't be as much as 'Banksters' get paid in the news," he laughed as his arm swung upwards to an image of a round faced bald-headed chubby character with fishy eyes. He was one of four bankers answering questions and sort of apologizing to Congress.

Mo Mus carried on: "If you take my advice you should think of banks as he does." He knew it would amuse the troops and it did. He smiled as laughter rippled through the air and he waited for quiet that came with scenes of yet more protests playing out on the silver screen.

The image showed credit alert flags with news that began to look the same after green, white and orange, and green, white and red flags for countries described as pigs with three more having the highest of all debt ratios compared to underlying GDP – Gross Domestic Product.

"We own sovereign debt. Their deficit reduction plans weaken their defenses while we advance credit to fund guerrilla lines of attack."

A white flag with a red leaf bordered in red appeared, followed by pictures of people objecting to identity theft that made them feel like sitting ducks. Reports compared home news to worsening debt crises overseas. Headlines announced the effectiveness of better banking guidelines and promoted confidence about good governance of banks the envy of the world. The Prime Compounder said it would be wrong to blame bankers for a dip in the economy that was not their fault.

"You will find many of our friends retire to Avalon," he said on cue.

Mo Mus went on: "It is up to you to choose where you want to live in retirement now the job is done." He spread his arms out with a shrug. "My work continues until I take my leave of the G20. You are welcome to stay in quarters for a month before G9 troops return from the field. Tomorrow you will be debriefed and given any assistance you may need to start new lives deserving of our souls."

The troops stood to attention while the General held the stance in a dutiful moment. His face softened and it looked as though he sort of showed compassion. "I am with you in your faith, I am very proud of you. I thank you, and I pray for your deliverance to Mammon."

Bad credit flags linked to newsbytes of public reaction to government spin on fewer public services and welfare benefit cutbacks. Troopers saw themselves saluting the General.

Soft music piped around the room and lights flickered in colors. Mo Mus handed over to a talented soldier in a DJ's alter ego, "OK, here we go with Trooper Lefty Chancit. Let the celebrations begin…"

The hall erupted into life and the music lifted and strobe lights flashed in beams that crisscrossed in wild patterns on globes in the ceiling.

General Mo Mus stepped off stage with his entourage to mingle with G8 people; most had not met for ten years, since basic training. The night was young and there was an endless supply of food and drink to feast on. There was plenty of talk with many financial advisors and accountants bragging about their most successful deals selling trick loans to old ladies known as 'Grannies' in the trade.

There was lots of talk about how they made off with loads of money.

The screen that had been filled with images of economic disaster was replaced with troopers in groups talking and dancing on smoke and mirrors. Drinks flowed and cameras switched from different angles with momentary shots of faces that if they saw themselves they would smile, and wave, and holler and hoot in a happy party mood.

Mo Mus Control to Major Won

Military celebrations didn't affect the debriefing schedule that started promptly at oh-eight-hundred hours. Every trooper was a special case, given a room number for a meeting with people interested in their deployment of the Tax Invaders Plan and their experience with rules of engagement where they worked. Major Won sat in Room 213.

"We need to discuss more about what happened in Confoundation."

"OK, what do you want to know?" Major Won J'Kobbs had nothing to fear. He knew how things worked and he had done his job.

"Confoundation has a fantastic reputation for highly regulated banks. The Fed Subprime Compounder promotes Ogstowne as a financial center to develop world class products for emerging markets. The MOB joined a trade mission in the East where we opened a center in Begone City. We have to lie low, but our ministers have to keep up appearances."

"What's that got to do with me?"

"Well, if it got out banks sold investments with tied loans it would expose our plan. You were recommended because in all of thirty-two billion, yours was the most difficult to follow the money."

Major Won wanted to get away and retire, "Who recommended me?"

"Don't know. Someone from the MOB from your time in '89." The recorder looked at his notes. "I expect you'll find out. They want to see you at ten-thirty in the Signature Room. It's along the main concourse, turn left for Section Eight."

Major Won knew where he had to be, and he knew he had time for a coffee in the cafeteria. He found the men's room and washed his face to freshen up. It had been a long night. He walked to the Signature Room and knocked on the door and he heard someone shout, "Enter!"

General Mo Mus looked up and waved him in to join two people with their backs to him from where they sat at a boardroom table. Major Won stepped forward and saluted the General who returned the formality still seated. "Easy Major, come in, take a pew," he gestured.

It was the obvious place to sit, next to the General and as he rounded the table he thought he recognized the MOB's lawyer. He stood for a moment to look and confirm a face farfetched in his mind.

The soldier recognized rank. "Major Ozegle?"

"Right," the lawyer said without smiling. They shook hands.

The General spoke: "Major Ozegle is a graduate from G7. He is in our Special Branch. I'd like you to meet Lurid Bison Ceboid, he is the Deputy Minister for the Confoundation Gallows Prosecutor."

"Pleased to meet you, sir." They shook hands over the table and Major Won took his place beside the General. He looked him in the eye and said, "What can I do for you sir?"

"We have a situation with the MOB. You remember the Kaleidoscope eighty-nine and ninety projects? The MOB got into a mess collecting a 'Sitting Duck' that became a 'Bombersuit'. We have to quash a counterclaim and see nothing like it happens again."

"Mmm I remember, but I didn't know Major Ozegle was one of us." He smiled as he measured the severity of the man across the table.

There was a knock at the door as another joined the meeting. Major Won looked up to see who else would be debriefed.

It was the MOB's Bræn Chyld, also ranked a Major.

The General welcomed him to the meeting with a quick introduction to continue the update. "When we developed the Tax Invaders Plan we realized we needed legal people as well as financial advisors and accountants. We had done quite well with bankers signing affidavits until the savings and loans fiasco. Do you know of the 'Caddysheik' deal that sent Ogstowne players and bankers to jail in the eighties?"

He looked at Major Won who said, "Yes sir, I remember it."

"We had to find a way to isolate bankers from loan documents. They signed affidavits for trick loans that left a paper trail. We had to review the experience to learn how to protect ourselves."

The General spoke quietly: "Lemon Broth figured out how to set up non-bank note credit default swaps tied to mortgage derivatives that put the onus on investors to prove banks collude with third parties."

Major Won knew this, but the General had to set the stage. He nodded to show he followed as Major Ozegle picked up the story.

"You remember when Major Chyld joined the MOB?"

There was no way he could have forgotten and he nodded as Major Ozegle continued. "He was the brains behind the L'Æmori affair. Fordo took the credit but he couldn't have done it without our Bræn. After he left the MOB, Cyn Fardo and Sully VanScrawl set up the ninety before yearend." He looked at Major Chyld.

Major Chyld confirmed the timing. "I was revolving through FCAC."

"We had problems with the eighty-nines," Major Ozegle explained. "It had to do with systems development. We requested postdated cheques that we posted to a common payment account. Each payment had to be processed manually, you see? The CCAP system upgrade 3.1 was behind schedule. And we had a problem with the rate of interest on notes that we had to change with order quantities. Cyn worked out a procedure to get them initialed in time. Do you remember?"

Major Chyld snorted. "Humph, I had to get Audit off his back."

"We thought it was okay, but Major Chyld left too soon." The lawyer looked vaguely across the table. "We created the ninety to test the rollout to start automatic payments. But it didn't work and Fordo had to use existing methods." He looked at the Deputy Minister and the General and then the Majors as if looking for sympathy.

Major Chyld leapt to a conclusion. "Don't tell me they mixed nineties with eight-nines until they got it fixed."

"Yep, it was a heck of a problem. We had to split nineties from eighty-nines to separate the loan payments. It wasn't fully automated until 4.0 when we litigated to collect nineties in default in ninety-six."

"Systems, huh?" Major Chyld understood problem with computers.

Then he asked, "How did you collect commingled loans?"

"Mmm…" Major Ozegle didn't say he exposed commingled loans to Robby Ducky. "It came out in litigation to collect an eighty-nine." He blamed the shortcomings of IT and it gave him the shudders.

"Is that why we're here?" Major Won wondered.

The General's answer sounded annoyed: "Yes, the MOB should have nipped Ducky's litigation in the bud. It's been a hell of a job to keep it quiet. The defendant and claimant is an author, he never stops writing. Every damn thing is a story to him. He's been published for it."

"I thought you had a grip on people like that, remember Furly Moat."

The Deputy Minister observed, "We do normally, but Ducky ran for office on consumer protection. Someone called him a 'Sitting Duck'; that got him going. He wasn't clever, just riled enough with truth to embarrass NDP politicians to launch Petition 44 for an investigation."

Major Chyld saw the problem and obvious solution. "So you put a gag order on him and the Confoundation ignored Petition 44, then what?"

"The MOB continued to collect what they started."

Major Chyld exhaled in exasperation. It made his lips reverberate: "Phewepple!" He looked at Major Ozegle. "I can't believe you kept litigating one loan." He could tell from his face to ask, "Why bother?"

"We had no choice. Ducky found the agency agreement and filed a counterclaim that L'Æmori decided to not defend. His lawyer filed a Note Default to defend against the alias company in another Court to keep it out of sight. They didn't tell him about it."

"So Ducky didn't know he could win by default judgment?"

"No. They told him he had to keep on finding evidence to defend the bank's claim for the first note. He wanted to settle several times, but the bank wouldn't allow it." Major Ozegle shrugged. "All the defending lawyers examined him but it didn't go well for us. He told the truth so we had nothing for a quick judgment. The MOB examined him three times."

Major Ozegle described the case. "It was a risk going to court to claim a loan in default with a Note Default to defend. Ducky had a strong counterclaim. He's a world-class JAD analyst and he figured how it worked from CCAP screens. There was only one account for commingled loans so he filed a claim the second note they couldn't defend either."

Major Won went, "Wow! Why didn't you accept his offer to settle?"

"It was a Mexican Standoff. The Court knew the MOB could win a claim but Ducky could win his counterclaim if L'Æmori didn't show in court." Major Ozegle flinched, "It's a nightmare. Defendants could blame the bank for irresponsible lending. It could expose the MOB to all kinds of claims, even to criminal charges being laid."

The lawyer was touchy about the thrust of his legal briefs on the table.

"I advised the MOB to keep litigating while the Avaloan Note Default to defend did the trick. We dragged it out for some six years. He had time to write three books. The more he wrote the more we had to fend off. He wrote the MOB Ombudsman, the Ombudsman for Investments, Anti-rackets, and Conjurer of Securities. They told him they couldn't follow up a case in litigation, so he complained about Al Fudgit selling securities to the Institute of Cheating Accountants, which fined him five thousand loonies. Then he filed a complaint with the Claw Society about Mykle L'Æmori notarizing signatures for bank loans that closed sales."

"What did the Claw Society say about L'Æmori?"

"They wrote there was nothing wrong with lawyers notarizing sworn affidavits." Major Ozegle raised his eyebrows and pursed his lips as he reflected on the consequences of Ducky's complaints.

"What made him write so much?" Major Won wondered out loud.

Minister Ceboid said, "His wife felt cheated and she supported him to get her money back. They analyzed it together and saw the big picture."

Major Won checked something: "So all this time his lawyer didn't tell him he was entitled to a default judgment to win his counterclaim?"

Major Ozegle had to admit it was true. "He had no idea. We thought he might find out, or that his lawyer might give the game away."

"Who was his lawyer?"

"Fright Fullman with Barnyard Oink and Associates."

"When was it heard?"

"We examined him three times, including Kaleidoscope, Mecory, Al Fudgit and the accounting firm. It made him ask why he couldn't examine the MOB, so he filed a motion to examine us." Major Ozegle didn't like it coming out. "He asked about six hundred questions that produced fifty-some refusals he followed up in court." The Major spread his hands on the table. "He recognized the writing on the note compared to Sully VanScrawl on loan charges that he had confirmed by handwriting analysis after examination. I told the judge there was no second note and denied litigating it to avoid a trial."

"Phew." Major Won remembered Sully VanScrawl's handiwork on his desk and realized the implication. "He proved an agency relationship with a Sully filling out a note to close a sale with commingled loans, which you had to deny to judges to avoid a trial. What next?"

"Fright panicked and quit. He told Ducky he wouldn't act if it meant he had to claim I lied in court. He quit as a professional courtesy."

"So the Oinks protected Kaleidoscope while they worked for Ducky?"

"Yes."

"Fright ended up protecting you, L'Æmori Avaloan and Fudgit?"

"Yes. His next lawyer Wire Tedd did the same until he quit as well."

"Bejeeze, what a screw-up." Major Won couldn't help himself. "You have to admire the Duckys. What next?" He wanted to know.

"Robby Ducky had to represent himself. He filed a motion to dismiss the bank's claim with a zero-cost-everyone-walks-away offer to drop his counterclaim and his wife's claim against the MOB et al."

"Good, so you accepted the offer and it was all over and done with."

Major Ozegle said simply, "No."

"No?"

"No, the bank rejected the offer and a judge refused to hear Ducky's motion. Justice Lang Donney said it was like *Alice in Wonderland* and threw it out. He wrote an order for Ducky to file his Factum and appear in Court to defend our motion for a summary judgment."

"In the face of all that, you went through with your claim?"

"Yes, we won." Major Ozegle glowered as if it was natural justice.

Major Won reprimanded: "You put our plan in public view."

"Ducky's ex-lawyer turned up in court with an abbreviated Factum for Defense to replace his own Factum for Defense and Counterclaim he had on file. Fright and I persuaded Justice Renta Horse to accept it rather than use Ducky's amended Factum.

I told the judge the handwriting analysis was not admissible and denied litigating the second note. We got the summary judgment we needed to collect."

"Robby Ducky must have complained about obstruction of justice."

"Mmm, the Claw Society wrote it wasn't my fault, but they chastized Fullman with an order to read a paper about the civility code."

"Did he appeal the ruling?"

"Yes, but Mdm Justice Lu'Squeeze told him, 'You could not have not known there was a bank loan.' Her ruling makes our loans legal."

"What about his counterclaim against Avaloan?"

"The court closed the file so it wasn't heard."

"No one told him to plead a judgment in default against L'Æmori to recover what he had to pay the MOB?" Major Chyld answered his own question with another: "Did he get a lawyer to litigate it?"

"No. Ducky still didn't know, and his new lawyer didn't litigate it."

"Did he pay the judgment?"

"We agreed to settle, but we missed making him sign a release to have the writs removed. The MOB still holds a lien on his house."

"You have a paid writ on his house you won't clear unless he drops his claim against the MOB and Avaloan defending the second note?"

"Avaloan's got it tied up in a lengthy Motion for Particulars. Ducky's lawyer didn't file his answers advising he had no need to prove he had a case for trial that would come out in discoveries."

"He's still wasting money on Confoundation lame duck lawyers?"

"Mmm, he's a glutton for punishment." Major Ozegle smiled thinly.

"I suppose they used the Note Default to defend against him?"

"Yes, they say Ducky didn't plead a default judgment on the first note because he never had a case. His next lawyer set him up with no evidence in court to prove he had no evidence in court for a judge to toss out the second claim."

"A judge threw it out?" Major Won stated the solution as a question.

"No, Ducky had a heart attack heading up to it. Wire decided it was a good time to get heavy on him to quit instead of going to court to prove a case for trial." Major Ozegle scratched his neck.

"So he signed a Notice to Discontinue?"

Major Ozegle looked pleased. "No, his lawyer got him to sign a proposal and the defendants can sue him if he doesn't quit."

Major Won summed up the legal battle. "Ducky proved the agency relationship. You resorted to perjury for the MOB to avoid a trial and his lawyer swapped factums for you to get a judgment. Even with a Note Default to defend, Ducky can't get a trial because his lawyer scotched a Motion for Particulars to make it easy for a judge to dismiss his claim. How much did they pay in legal fees to beat him down?"

Major Ozegle shrugged. "The MOB paid about a million. Half again for defendants' lawyers. He paid Oink a hundred thousand."

"You made a killing on perjury and extortion to obstruct justice."

Major Ozegle denied the bank's legal tactics. "It's not extortion."

"You're holding paid writs on his house as ransom. His new lawyer intimidated him to sign a proposal when he was sick to get his house back. Wouldn't you say the bank is afraid of Robby Ducky?"

Major Ozegle bridled. "If you put it that way."

Deputy Minister Ceboid was getting impatient. "The point is how we make sure the Tax Invasion Plan continues?"

The General took charge and confirmed the reason for Major Won being there. "You implemented the plan for L'Æmori. You have field experience. What do we have to do to silence Robby Ducky?"

Major Won thought it through. The room went still as they waited for his conclusion. He took his time as the General knew his approach to solving problems. Major Ozegle wanted to speak but Mo Mus gave him a withering look. He had confidence in his Major Won.

Major Won spoke, he had their attention. "The problem comes down to Robby Ducky having too much time to think," he said. "Robby Ducky wasn't messing with you. You were messing with his mind. You told him our game rules. He had to tell you everything he discovered. It's in court records. He had to write what he learned. It was all he could do. He didn't know his own lawyers would betray him as much as they did. He didn't know the Secret Claw Society would protect them to such extremes as they had to in your case."

Major Ozegle took offense. He looked sullen and bit his tongue.

"Ducky had faith in truth you desperately had to cover with lies to avoid a trial. He's a whistleblower and he had a blind faith in justice denied to him by his own lawyers." Major Won looked at Lurid Bison Ceboid, who nodded as the team followed his reasoning.

"You told him our plan and he wrote his story to be judged. He had the evidence and was traumatized by intimidation and injustice." Major Won continued to analyze. "The bank and the defendants' lawyers, even the lawyers he paid for ganged up and legalized him to death."

He paused a moment. "The police let him down, and he became afraid of the justice system that refused to admit evidence for a trial. Judges penalized him with costs every time he appeared and lost in court."

Major Won decided to test the bank's lawyer. "He'd be better dead."

Major Ozegle took the bait. "He was told his life was on the line."

Deputy Ceboid interjected. "He was too well known as an advocate, he ran for office. He started Petition 44 for consumer protection. He spoke on television. People took pictures of him with world leaders, even presidents. He presented court records as a Confoundation Case for Banking Reform on a summer's day at the White House."

Major Won smiled at the reaction. "No, I mean for his own good, you attacked his conscience, he couldn't live with himself. Every time you knocked him down, he found the moral fiber to get up and fight."

"Humph!" Major Ozegle knew it; ha had aged with Robby Ducky.

"All your legal arguments confirmed the truth he thought he could use in court, or public debate to set him free. Hmm?"

Major Ozegle shielded as a consummate lawyer. "He wouldn't lie down. He wrote complaints about lawyers. He wrote the government that we swapped his Factum to fool judges to obstruct justice."

"That's his story. It's about truth and justice. He had to write to make sense out of lunacy to keep sane. He had to connect the dots. That's the problem, you made a writer of all people think about dream laws and politics for bankers, day after day, for ten years."

Major Ozegle argued for Mammon: "We had no choice. We had to crush him to protect the MOB from cross-claims. We can't let Ducky win by default. It'd start a class action. We have to hold a lien on his house as ransom." He looked desperate. "What else can we do?"

"How long did it take Ducky to figure it out as a system, six years?"

Major Ozegle had to admit to a long time. "He said it took him three months to reconstruct CCAP. If he hadn't got an order to examine the MOB he wouldn't have recognized Sully VanScrawl on the second note." He thought of Ducky's persistence. "When Avaloan abused procedure with five hundred questions for a trial they asked him to prove there was a mortgage. So he looked for it. It was in…"

Major Won sat up. "He found our… Kaleidoscope's mortgage?"

"Yes, the Claw Society followed up his complaint about Fright who wrote the mortgage was a total loss to investors in his reply. It made Ducky focus. He woke up Christmas Eve ten years after we started to collect and found the deed of sale, the mortgage and L'Æmori's Consignment of Rent to the holders for a loony. It was in Gofa's file the Conjurer closed years ago. Ducky said it was a gift from God."

"Had to be." Major Won shook his head. "It was pretty well hidden."

Major Ozegle said, "Yes well, he complained to the Claw Society with a demand they report Oink to the police for withholding evidence and interfering with court procedures to obstruct justice. We had to put pressure on him and his wife to quit when he reported L'Æmori for handling trick loans with criminal intent to defraud the Queen. He had found everything his lawyers withheld from court. They told him to find the smoking gun, which is exactly what he did… in the end."

"That's the point, in the end," Major Won reflected. "We can't allow the Tax Invaders Plan to go in a book on trial for people to read. You need a truth embargo that's quicker than lawyers fooling judges that mess with jurisprudence." He looked at Major Ozegle, and then his General Mo Mus. "It will be safer for you if you cut civil statutes of limitations from six years to two. It would stop a whistle-blower replaying bank loan game-rules-for-sitting-ducks for sure." He reinforced his conclusion, "It'd quash all kinds of litigation, eh?"

The General slapped the table and leaned back in his chair to address the government. "Brilliant! There you have it, Lurid, a two-year statute of limitations to serve Mammon. You know what to do, right?"

Silver Bullet Reverse Onus Rule

Most Majestic Mastiff Badio Dinwuddy
Summary Judiciary of the Confoundation and Great Divide
and Master Fouter of the Central Agency for Collections
(All praise the Gallows Prosecutor).

Your Most Majestic Mastiff

I, Robby Ducky, in humility and gratefulness for the honor to write my story, do hereby bestow myself upon sympathetic readers to close with pleadings for relief from bad bank loans and endless prosecution.

In that I have always complied with the will of Confoundation Tax Law (Hail our Sharper Leader) I beseech you consider my sorry state. I confess that from time to time I have taken leave of my mind to join confabs in rarified atmospheres with creatures well above my station.

Flights of fancy whisked me away from my cabal as splendid as it is (All praise the Gallows Prosecutor) to even finer conference facilities and sumptuous junkets where I met Robber Barons and dined with world leaders to discuss a responsible lending *'Reverse Onus Rule'*.

Indeed, it easy to stand on either side of a mirror in my mind that separates fact from fiction. Am I on the same page as former Prime Minister Gordon Brown espousing *'Capitalism without Capital'* as a cause of debt sworn in my name? Or, am I in tune with law enforcers blind to potentially criminal acts given judges rule bank documents prove no credible evidence for trial concerning *'Sitting Duck'* loans?

In fairness that is the jurisprudence way in Confoundation (Hail our Sharper Leader) excluding the L'Æmori example that breaks the rule, game players that cheat have been punished. (All praise the Shadow Chancellor, the Supreme Prosecutor, and the Chief Proctor). To wit:

A loans officer has been fined a hundred thousand loonies for forging clients' signatures. An agent for the bank known by various aliases has been fined sixty-five thousand for accredited investor failings. An accountant has been found guilty and fined five thousand for taking referral fees from loans to sell investments to accounting clients and also fined forty-five thousand in a precedent setting case for taking secret commissions selling an 'Art-flip' variant of tax shelter schemes.

Unanswered letters hide dark secrets. A police file not numbered and closed, and a court with numbered files never actually closed. Such are my delusions from the uncertainties of unreported testimony given in endless litigation a Justice of Peace might consider 96-CU-115730 CM is a Catch22 precedent to legalize the *'Reverse Onus Rule'*.

The bank that sued me for years to collect a loan based on my wife's stolen identity also sued the accountant involved for an exact same investment loan set up in his wife's name. The matter was set aside after the accountant's lawyer turned the table on the bank to prove its loan. Had the case gone to court, the defendant might have testified how he received a commission from the plaintiff/bank having sworn witness to family monikers for a pre-approved loan paid to the bank's agent taking the oath for credit used to close the insider's deal.

Could a bank operative con artist use a *'Reverse Onus Rule'* to outwit a bank? A Public Information might unravel crime woven in a modus operandi: Concealed Encumbrances 385(1), Market Pricing S380(2), Identity Theft 402.2(1) and Trafficking 402.2(2), False Oaths 131(1) and 134(1), Secret Commissions 426(1), and lawyers in a court record apparently interfering with procedure to obstruct justice with perjury and extortion thrown in to avoid trial, 137 and 139(1).

A spin-off consumer protection junta in Confoundation does not stop a bank refusing to clear paid writs held in ransom for a signature to release them from my wife's lawsuit, which the bank denied they were litigating to avoid trial. It feels like extortion as I revolve in a Fiscal Stability Asylum that has no jurisdiction over bank operations except for writing laws to authorize money lies in Wonderland.

Would that I might stop having to fend off motions with the gracious consent of the Supreme Judiciary endorsing intervener status in this affair (All praise the Gallows Prosecutor). I trust eleven years bound in court without trial to account for wrongdoings at the behest of the Supreme Overseer might be taken into consideration to justify relief. (All praise the Shadow Chancellor, and the Chief Proctor.)

Yours with due respect and humbleness, and forever in your debt,

R Ducky

ABCP Crisis in Canada

NDP Queen's Park Petition 44
Taxpayer Protection
Banking Reforms

Gullible client *'Signature-Specific-Identity-Theft'* experience with Bank of Montreal and Allied Canadian *'Ponzi'* tax shelter loans.

NDP Petition 44 'Reverse Onus Rule' discussion paper to protect taxpayers from 'Toxic' loans that without regulation can be laundered through taxation systems and bankrupt financial conduits in default.

Sir John Vickers, Chair of the ICB - Independent Commission on Banking
Victoria House, Southampton Row, London WC1B 4AD
(feedback@bankingcommission.gsi.gov.uk)

March 28, 2011

Dear Sir John,

Subject: My husband *'Gullible Client'* case for a *'Silver Bullet'* Retail and Investment Banking *'Reverse Onus Rule'*.
Ref: The Daily Telegraph March 5, 2011: Mr. Mervyn King asserts banks target *'gullible clients'* for quick profits.
Ref: The Guardian March 17, 2011: *'Lord Turner seeks eternal vigilance over banks'* to control *'exotic'* activities.

Further to your January 22, 2011 speech at the London Business School comparing regulations for retail versus investment banking, I refer to my experience as a British citizen with Bank of Montreal re Mr. Mervyn King the Governor of the Bank of England's caution banks target so-called *'gullible clients'* for profit, and Lord Turner's heedful warning to *regulate shadow banking to ensure new risks do not emerge outside mainstream banking*.

I attach a JAD – Joint Application Design business process analysis of a BMO lending technology my accountant apparently used to receive a secret commission for false witness of my signature for an unsigned, undocumented, undisclosed loan in my name to sell a tax sheltered SIV – Structured Investment Vehicle to my husband.

JAD is a business process analysis technique that specifies prototypes to develop computer systems. I used it to model an *'Off-site Loans Closings'* that BMO litigated against my husband for ten years until a judge ruled one of two commingled loans in one account in my name was properly documented for summary judgment to collect.

The workflow illustrates *'Step-transaction-daylight-loans'* for a *'credit-default-swap-mortgage-derivative'* sold as an RRSP – Registered Retirement Savings Plan. It traces my passage into debt to a bank seemingly involved in a scheme geared to generate claims for rent taken to repay mortgage interest as losses to defraud taxpayers.

My JAD translates BMO lending practices to point-form language that connects the dots in front-line sales and a back office accreditation system to sell investments and pay commissions to sales reps who witness signatures on notes that close sales. BMO gave evidence that their agent notarized an *'Affidavit of Subscribing Witness'* to fill out a PLSA – Personal Loan Service Application, in my case without my SIN – Social Insurance Number or my signature. The loan history log shows the bank presumed I had income without verification. Handwriting analysis indicates a bank employee filled out a demand note to evidence a loan with no value received, or benefit to me.

Despite the RCMP citing potential criminal acts, an appeal court ruled my husband could **not** have not known he had a bank loan *(in my name)*. It was a highly visible case in 2009 with political interest in a *'Reverse Onus Rule'* that my husband discussed with the Canadian government to promote at the White House for G20 debate… *that lenders must prove identity validation and financial due diligence before transacting loans to collect*.

I understand the ICB reviews public input and I enclose a cash flow analysis to illustrate the hidden risk of ABCP – Asset Backed Commercial Paper that is still **not regulated**. The problem is my husband signed a loan dependant commercial paper as a *'Maker'* of a worthless non-bank note that gave notional *'mortgage'* value to the *'Holder'*. The serious issue is the *monetization of toxic loans though taxation systems*. BMO had no right to fabricate credit in my name. It seems BMO was more conniving than my husband gullible. *How could I have prevented my debt for his part in the largest $32 billion bankruptcy of a shadow banking financial conduit in Canadian history?*

Sir John, *my husband was duped into making sense fake money!* Please address the risk of potentially criminal ABCP Third Party Notes in bank regulations. Will you protect the private and public wealth of British taxpayers, the same as the New Democratic Party reading Petition 44 at Queen's Park, Toronto intends for Canadians?

Yours sincerely,

Jill Crawford.

Att. ABCP: Model, Mortgage, Consignment, Cash Flow, JAD Workflow, Connecting the Dots, RCMP Citation, Canadian Law, WSJ Report
cc. Mr. Mervyn King, Governor of the Bank of England. enquiries@bankofengland.co.uk
cc. Lord Turner, Chairman of the Financial Services Authority. consumer.queries@fsa.gov.uk
cc Mr. Mark Carney, Governor of the Bank of Canada info@bankofcanada.ca
cc. Hon. James Flaherty, Minister of Finance Canada jflaherty@fin.gc.ca, fina@parl.gc.ca
cc Hon. Jack Layton, Leader NDP jack@fed.ndp.ca; laytoj@parl.gc.ca, and Hon. Andrea Howath, ahorwath-qp@ndp.on.ca

Globe Investor

INVESTOR'S EDGE

Michael Emory of Allied Properties stands in the lobby of their new offices on Adelaide St., Toronto. ASHLEY HUTCHESON FOR THE GLOBE AND MAIL

Old is gold for Toronto-based trust

Allied Properties' brick-and-beam office buildings a bright spot in darkening sector

BY LORI McLEOD
REAL ESTATE REPORTER TORONTO

A company that discovered its business strategy in adverse times, office landlord **Allied Properties Real Estate Investment Trust** offers a way to invest in the ongoing revitalization of city centres.

The largest owner of brick-and-beam office buildings in Canada, Allied has a portfolio of 69 character-filled low-rises in downtown Toronto, Montreal, Quebec City and Winnipeg.

"This is very clearly a long-term play on urbanization," said Neil Downey, managing director at RBC Dominion Securities, which has an "outperform" rating on the units. "There's also something to be said for a company that can survive tough times versus one that starts up when things are easy."

The REIT, which went public in 2003, struggled in the late 1980s as a buyer of small storefront retail properties. Overbuilding and too much debt sent the commercial real estate industry into an abysmal downturn in the early 1990s.

But despite the 20-per-cent vacancy rate in its overall property portfolio, Allied discovered gold in two funky office buildings it owned at Yonge & Front in downtown Toronto, which remained steadfastly full. "We liked what we saw there, and I think it put us at the leading edge of the current movement toward

densification," said chief executive officer Michael Emory.

The idea of encouraging people to return to the city to live and work has taken hold this decade, and feels more like a permanent change in attitude than a trend, he added.

Allied's turn-of-the-century oldies, now known in the industry as Class I buildings, have much lower tax and operating costs than sleek downtown skyscrapers. Many needed serious facelifts to restore them to their former glory, leading to lucrative rent hikes for Allied. "In effect, he created a new asset class over the past decade," Mr. Downey said of Mr. Emory.

After going public in 2003 to raise capital for acquisitions, Allied has purchased more properties in Toronto, along with Montreal, Quebec City and Winnipeg. Attracted by lower rents and features including exposed brick and bright, high-ceilinged spaces, firms including animators, designers and ad agencies have flocked there.

At the end of 2007, Allied's space was 97.9-per-cent full, with many buildings occupied by a few, large tenants.

The global credit crunch has made it next to impossible for real estate buyers to get financing, but Allied recently obtained a mortgage for two new property acquisitions at a rate lower than its average of 5.6 per cent. "Things definitely have changed, and we had to

accept a shorter term than we would have liked. However, out of 12 potential lenders, we had six pretty good options, and that demonstrates the market is far from dead," Mr. Emory said.

Allied usually makes individual building acquisitions in the $15-million to $30-million range. As the market for financing gets tighter, this focus on smaller deals is working to the company's advantage, a sea change from the past few years when it had to bundle its purchases together to get attention from lenders.

But the company is not immune to the jitters spreading through the market as industry watchers try to gauge how much pain is yet to come out of the U.S.

"I am concerned about the prospect of a deeper U.S. slowdown. Nobody's decoupled, and our business is directly correlated to the general economy," Mr. Emory said. "Having said that, past experience suggests we can fare pretty well in a downturn."

Another risk to the company's outlook includes new office supply that will hit the Toronto market starting in 2009, and has the potential to cause a decrease in rents. With REIT prices depressed, the company would also be hard-pressed to go back to the market for funding if it found a very large acquisition opportunity. Allied's units are down 9 per cent this year.

Allied Properties REIT

SHARE PRICE, DAILY CLOSE, (AP.UN–TSX)

Friday's close
$18.79, down 16¢

A M J J A S O N D J F
2007   2008
SOURCE: THOMSON DATASTREAM

Allied will continue to look for acquisitions in its core markets, and would also consider Halifax and Vancouver if the right opportunities came up. It will also try to find ways to make better use of existing properties by building both "out and up," Mr. Emory said.

In its last reported quarter, ended September, 2007, Allied's funds from operations rose by 55 per cent year-over-year to $10.4-million. Distributable income rose by 80 per cent to $10.9-million, while its payout ratio dropped to 72 per cent from 84 per cent.

In the past three years, Allied has raised its distribution payment to unitholders on the anniversary of its initial public offering, which took place two weeks ago. With financial results due Friday, Mr. Emory was unable to comment on whether history will repeat itself, but said Allied plans to keep its payout ratio in the conservative 75 per cent range.

MANUFACTURED DEBT OBLIGATIONS TO ABCP THIRD PARTY NOTES

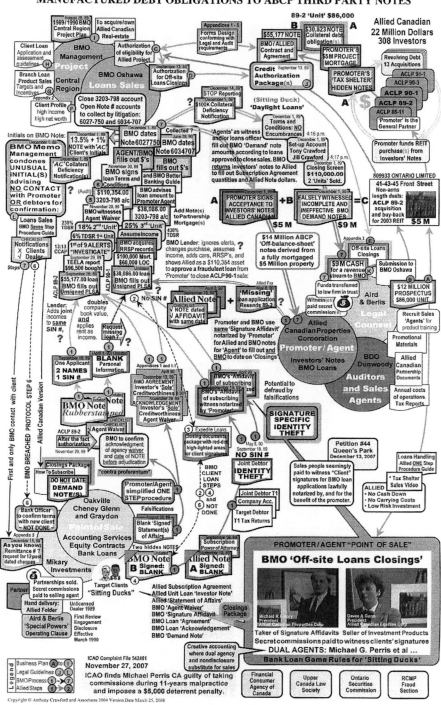

Pre-Executed Step Transaction Ponzi Tax Credit Savings Loans

Step Transaction Toxic Loans: The following step transaction illustrates front and back office operations reselling mortgages on income producing commercial real estate as investments that cannot be sold or function without codependent loans that report interest to process claims for personal income tax credits.

Pre-executed Bank Loans: Sales start with prospective income tax credit savers signing so-called '*packages*' of documents shown. Front office sales reps swear paid witness to signatures notarized by the investment '*Promoter*' who as agent of the bank confirms people signing Subscription Agreements and Non-bank Notes are persons of the same name indebted to pre-executed bank loans applying for money to invest. The packages are sent to the underwriter's back office with agency waivers for accreditations where the bank rubberstamps its logo on signed but otherwise blank Bank-demand Notes to collect.

Off-site Loans Closings: The back office fills out PLSA – Personal Loan Service Applications that with notarized '*Affidavits of Subscribing Witness*' need not be signed or disclosed. On closings the bank fills out its demand notes in amounts for units sold afforded to investors' personal credit worthiness's. The bank dates the notes and advances borrowed amounts to the front office. Each transaction '*papers*' notional principal to each Non-bank Note that the agent for the bank signs in acceptance of '*real*' money thereof to create mortgage derivative credit default swap ABCP – Asset Backed Commercial Paper that performs as an SIV – Structured Investment Vehicle. Each SIV has the sole purpose of holding assets and issuing claims against them. In this case, mortgage interest to claim for income-tax credits.

Mortgage in Default: The following tax scheme continues to launder worthless bank loan dependent ABCP Third Party Notes through taxation systems until the mortgage is at end of term, or in default. In this event, the bank and its agent as the DIP – Debtor in Possession collect principal amounts to clear the loans and mortgage to reacquire the property shown in the attached paper trail and cash flow analysis.

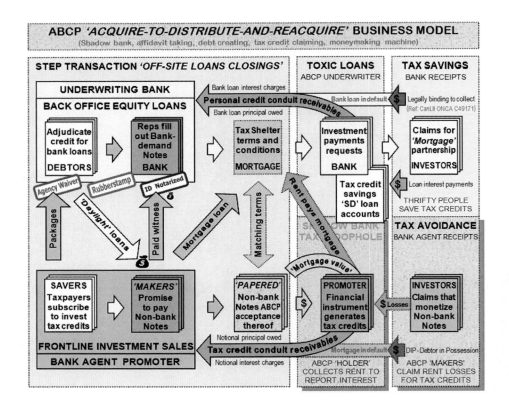

ABCP 'ACQUIRE-TO-DISTRIBUTE-AND-REACQUIRE' BUSINESS MODEL
(Shadow bank, affidavit taking, debt creating, tax credit claiming, moneymaking machine)

Financial Conduits: The tax avoidance scheme is geared to generate a tax saving financial conduit for the benefit of the bank and a tax avoidance financial conduit for the benefit of the investment dealer. After '*Closings*' the bank confirms its terms and conditions in the first and only contact by the bank about lending to investors: '*As you know the bank provided equity financing for your Tax Shelter unit purchase and we are pleased to confirm the details of your investment loan.*' The bank requests payments to start a flow of cash to pay interest on debt in tax credit savings loan accounts for as long as the mortgage exists. The dealer as the '*Holder*' of Non-bank Notes signed by each investor as its '*Maker*' collects and reports rent that pays the interest on the mortgage for investors to claim '*income losses*' as personal expenses for addition so-called '*Mortgage Partnership*' tax credits.

184

US Tax Law: In the US, the IRS – Internal Revenue Service has issued a public warning, '***Abusive trust arrangements will not produce the tax benefits advertised by their promoters***'. The IRS and the FBI – Federal Bureau of Investigations is concerned about the long-term effects in world economies. In 2005, the Senate Permanent Subcommittee on Investigations defined abusive shelters, '***Transactions in which a significant purpose is the avoidance or evasion of federal, state or local tax in a manner not intended by the law***'. The following charts illustrate the effect of ABCP Third Party Notes that generate ongoing tax credit losses at government expense until mortgage default in the largest failure of a financial conduit in Canadian history with $32 billion in bailouts and an estimated $85 billion debt collection by the banks.

PONZI TAX CREDIT LOANS

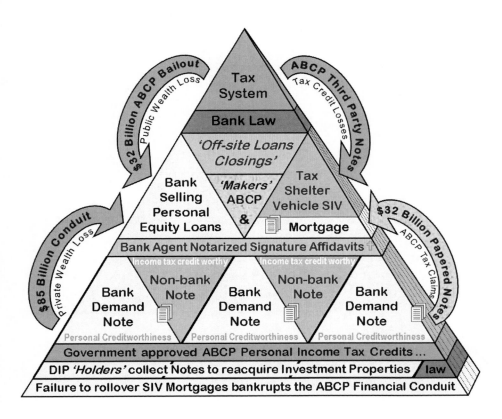

'OFF-SITE LOANS CLOSINGS' STEP TRANSACTION

Manufactured Debt Obligations to Rubberstamped and Papered Notes

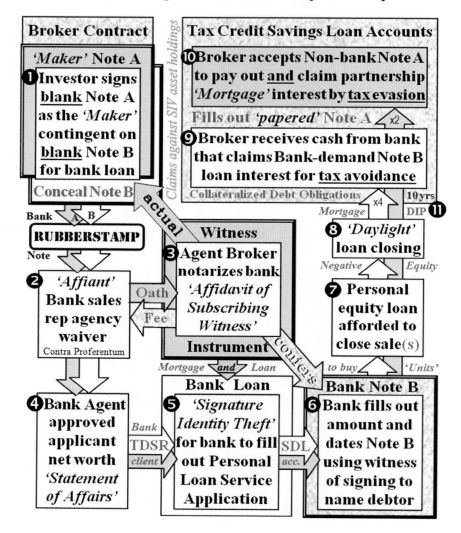

Broker Contract

'Maker' Note A

❶ Investor signs **blank** Note A as the *'Maker'* contingent on **blank** Note B for bank loan

Conceal Note B

Claims against SIV asset holdings

Tax Credit Savings Loan Accounts

❿ Broker accepts Non-bank Note A to pay out <u>and</u> claim partnership *'Mortgage'* interest by <u>tax evasion</u>

Fills out *'papered'* Note A x2

❾ Broker receives cash from bank that claims Bank-demand Note B loan interest for <u>tax avoidance</u>

Collateralized Debt Obligations   10yrs

Bank A B

RUBBERSTAMP

Note

❷ *'Affiant'* Bank sales rep agency waiver

Contra Proferentum

actual

Witness

❸ Agent Broker notarizes bank *'Affidavit of Subscribing Witness'*

Oath

Fee

Instrument

Mortgage x4 DIP ⓫

❽ *'Daylight'* loan closing

Negative   Equity

❼ Personal equity loan afforded to close sale(s)

confers

Mortgage *and* Loan

Bank Loan

❺ *'Signature Identity Theft'* for bank to fill out Personal Loan Service Application

Bank
TDSR
client

to buy   *'Units'*

Bank Note B

❻ Bank fills out amount and dates Note B using witness of signing to name debtor

❹ Bank Agent approved applicant net worth *'Statement of Affairs'*

SDL
acc.

(4) VHIS 3142   History Inquiry   3LA3 05/06/90 10:43
SUMMATION: BASED ON OUR CLIENT'S GOOD N.W @ $687M (TNW @ $536M) TDSR @ 25%
WE RECOMMEND 1) EXIST CREDIT BE CONFIRMED AS IS 2) PROPOSAL OF ADD $38,086.00
ALL TACS OF ACLP90-1 / /89-2 TOTAL $2963.00 -OR- 25% ALTHOUGH WIFE'S INCOME IS NOT
VERIFIED FOR 1989, WE HAVE USED A MIN FIG OF $50M FOR THE YEAR FOR TDSR

(3) AFFIDAVIT OF SUBSCRIBING WITNESS

I, MICHAEL FERRIS , of the City of Oakville
in the Province of Ontario . Make oath and say:
I am subscribing witness to the attached instrument(s) and
I was present and saw it/them executed at Oakville Ont by
JILL & ANTHONY CRAWFORD
I verily believe the each person whose signature I witnessed
is the party of the same name referred to in the instrument.

SWORN before me at the City of)
Oakville   in the)   WITNESS
Province of   Ontario   )
this   8   day of May , 19 90)
SPECIMEN SIGNATURE OF CLIENT   A COMMISSIONER FOR TAKING AFFIDAVITS

Bank of Montreal ■■ Banque de Montreal

Bank of Montreal
Loan Transmittal Form
Transmission de prêt
291 Oshawa, Ont.   Crawford A/g

LOAN TYPE   □ PLP   □ RRP   □ HOL/PLOC   □ FCR
TYPE DE PRET   □ CPP   □ PR   MOVEMENT   RCP
AMOUNT/MONTANT $ 38,086

PLC Processing Requirements (Lender to Complete)

Personal Statement of Affairs as at the ___ day of ___, 19__.
__ Mr. __ Dr. __ Miss __ Mrs.   D. M. Y.   __ Married __ Single
ANTHONY CRAWFORD   Date of Birth   Name of Spouse
Name
Home Address   Home Telephone
I Presently:__ Own __ Rent __ Other   Residence
(if owned is registered in the name of)

Previous Address (if less than 3 yrs)

Name of Employer

Business Address

Previous Employer (if less than 1 yr)

Employment Income + Other
(please provide proof of Total Income

Business Bankers Name and Phone

Accountants Name and Phone Numb

STATEMENT OF ASSETS & LIA
ASSETS Estima
Cash
Stocks
Mutual Funds
R.R.S.P.'s
Real Estate
Summary of Tax Shelter
Investment/details listed (A) on reverse)
Other Assets
Automobiles
Current Tax Liability: $
NET WORTH $ Total Assets $ Total Liabilities $
Bank Information: Name and Address of your main Bank(s) (Include Account No.)
REAL ESTATE DETAILS
Estimated Market Value   How Registered   Purchase Price   Year of Purchase   Outstanding Liability
TAX SHELTER INVESTMENTS
Name of Partnership   Estimated Market Value (A)   Amount of Equity Loan (B)   Monthly Payments (C)
Name/Address of Lender
TOTAL OF: (A) $ (B) $ (C) $

- Please ensure that these sections are completed accurately
- Please transfer TOTALS of A, B, and C to Summary of Tax Shelter Investments on the front page indicated.

CONTINGENT LIABILITIES (if any)
Amount   Name of Primary Debtor   Name
INSURANCE
Amount   Type   Insurer
WITNESS: SIGNATURE OF APPLICANT:
NOTE:
I authorize Allied Canadian Equities Corporation to obtain cred
I certify that all information in this Application is true and
financial institution to determine my creditworthiness. I agree
to, receive from, and share and exchange with others, including
have financial dealings, credit and other information about me.

Copy of RRSP, F/S

I have completed and enclosed all documents as indicated above and acknowledge responsibility for their correct completion.
Ian Forbes

(5) **Bank of Montreal**
1-3 Oshawa, Ont.   Branch

(1) Bank of Montreal
(2) **(6)** June 29, 90. 38,086

the sum of Thirty eight thousand + eighty six xx
1.0
and to pay interest monthly at a rate of ___ per cent per annum above the Bank of Montreal's prime interest
rate per annum in effect from time to time, up to and after maturity, compounded monthly from the due date of such interest until actual payment
at the above mentioned branch of the Bank of Montreal. At the date of this note such prime interest rate per annum is 14.75
Value received.

On demand I promise to pay for

Bank of Montreal ■■ Banque de Montreal
2351
8803-78 Jan 17/9
Crawford
C Suft   15

(8)
Jan 90   1370.78
Feb 90
Mar 90
Apr 90
May   6027
June   X 50   75
July   X 100
Aug
Sep   X 25
Oct
Nov
Dec

The First Canadian Bank ■■ La Première Banque Canadienne
Bank of Montreal ■■ Banque de Montreal
Confirmation of Bank Charges
Confirmation des frais bancaires   Feb 27 19 91
In response to your recent request, the Bank of Montreal confirms the following
Bank Charges paid during the year 19 ___.
351 Oshawa Main   90-2

Principal of Loan
et emprunt $ 14,710.73   Investment # 8027 750

MR ANTHONY CRAWFORD
761 LAKESHORE RD W
OAKVILLE
ONT L6K 1G4   for 90-1   Investment #
2826.70

(9)

(7) ORIGINAL - Lender Copy

INVESTOR NOTE

FOR VALUE RECEIVED, the undersigned (herein called the 'Maker') hereby promises to pay to or to the order of Allied Canadian Ltd Partnership (90-1) or
any subsequent holder of this promissory note (herein called the 'Holder') at its office in Toronto (or such other place as the Holder may designate)

a) the principal sum of $46,914 multiplied by 1 (herein called 'the number of interest(s) subscribed for by the Maker') in lawful currency of Canada
(herein called the 'Principal')

b) interest in like money on the unpaid portion from time to time of the Principal until November 1, 1991, at the rate of 10.875 per annum, calculated monthly

IN WITNESS WHEREOF Allied Canadian Properties Corporation has executed this acceptance and acknowledgement the ___ day of June 1990

By ___   c.s. Witness ___   Signature of Maker ___   General Partner, 809980, Ontario Limited

(10)

Charge/Mortgage of Land

Province of Ontario

Form 2 — Land Registration Reform Act, 1984

902645   2.13

NUMBER CT 902645 CERTIFICATE OF REGISTRATION 30 SEP 1987 2.13 A.M. TORONTO NO. 63 TORONTO J. L. Haughey LAND REGISTRAR New Property Identifiers Additional See Schedule ☐ Executions Additional See Schedule ☐	(1) Registry ☒ Land Titles ☐ (2) Page 1 of 4 pages

(3) Property Identifier(s) Block   Property   Additional See Schedule ☐

(4) Principal Amount Five Million Two Hundred Thousand------------ ----------------------xx/100 Dollars $ 5,200,000.00

(5) Description

FIRSTLY
In the City of Toronto, in the Municipality of Metropolitan Toronto and being composed of Part of Water Lot M, or 33 and Part of Water Lot L, or 32 and Part of the "Walks and Gardens" south of Front Street as more particularly described firstly in Schedule "A" attached hereto.
SECONDLY
In the City of Toronto, in the Municipality of Metropolitan Toronto and being composed of part of Water Lot "A" opposite Town Lot "A" and also a part of the Walks and Gardens property as more particularly described Secondly in Schedule "A" attached hereto.

(6) This Document Contains (a) Redescription New Easement Plan/Sketch ☐ (b) Schedule for: Description ☒ Additional Parties ☐ Other ☒

(7) Interest/Estate Charged Fee Simple

(8) Standard Charge Terms — The parties agree to be bound by the provisions in Standard Charge Terms filed as number 875 and the Chargor(s) hereby acknowledge(s) receipt of a copy of these terms.

(9) Payment Provisions

(a) Principal Amount $ 5,200,000.00	(b) Interest Rate 11.0 % per annum	(c) Calculation Period semi-annually
(d) Interest Adjustment Date Y 1987 M 10 D 01	(e) Payment Date and Period 1st monthly	(f) First Payment Date Y 1987 M 11 D 01
(g) Last Payment Date 1997 10 01	(h) Amount of Each Payment Fifty Thousand and Fifty-One Dollars ---------------57/100 Dollars $ 50,051.57	
(i) Balance Due Date 1997 10 01	(j) Insurance full insurable value Dollars $	

(10) Additional Provisions   Continued on Schedule ☐

(11) Chargor(s) The chargor hereby charges the land to the chargee and certifies that the chargor is at least eighteen years old and that

The chargor(s) acknowledge(s) receipt of a true copy of this charge.

Name(s)	Signature(s)	Date of Signature Y M D
MARKET BLOCK TORONTO PROPERTIES LTD., IN TRUST	Per: Andrew M. Clarke, President	1987 09 30

(12) Spouse(s) of Chargor(s) I hereby consent to this transaction.

Name(s)	Signature(s)	Date of Signature Y M D

(13) Chargor(s) Address for Service 116 Yorkville Avenue, Toronto, Ontario M5R 1C2

(14) Chargee(s)

THE PRUDENTIAL INSURANCE COMPANY OF AMERICA

(15) Chargee(s) Address for Service 200 Consilium Place, Scarborough, Ontario M1H 3E6 Attn: Real Estate Investment Office

(16) Assessment Roll Number of Property Cty. Mun. Map Sub. Par. MULTIPLE

(17) Municipal Address of Property	(18) Document Prepared by:	Fees
41, 43 and 45 Front Street East Toronto, Ontario	Phillip P. Macdonald Woolley, Dale & Dingwall P.O. Box 65 Toronto-Dominion Centre Toronto, Ontario M5K 1E7	Registration Fee $16 Total

Document General
Form 4 — Land Registration Reform Act, 1984

902729 2·6 D

NUMBER CT 902729

CERTIFICATE OF REGISTRATION

30 SEP 1987 A.M.

TORONTO
NO. 63
TORONTO

J. L. Haughey

LAND REGISTRAR

New Property Identifiers
Additional See Schedule ☐

Executions
Additional See Schedule ☐

---

(1) Registry ☒   Land Titles ☐   (2) Page 1 of 6 pages

(3) Property Identifier(s)   Block   Property   Additional See Schedule ☐

(4) Nature of Document
CONDITIONAL ASSIGNMENT OF RENTALS

(5) Consideration
OTHER GOOD AND VALUABLE CONSIDERATION AND THE
SUM OF ONE DOLLAR---------- Dollars $ 1.00

(6) Description FIRSTLY
In the City of Toronto, in the Municipality of Metropolitan
Toronto and being composed of Part of Water Lot M, or 33
and Part of Water Lot L, or 32 and Part of the "Walks and
Gardens" south of Front Street as more particularly
described firstly in Schedule "A" attached hereto.
SECONDLY
In the City of Toronto, in the Municipality of Metropolitan
Toronto and being composed of part of Water Lot "A"
opposite Town Lot "A" and also a part of the Walks and
Gardens property as more particularly described
Secondly in Schedule "A" attached hereto.

(7) This Document Contains:
(a) Redescription New Easement Plan/Sketch ☐
(b) Schedule for: Description ☒ Additional Parties ☐ Other ☒

This Document provides as follows:

Executed Conditional Assignment of Rentals attached hereto as Schedule "B".

Continued on Schedule ☐

This Document relates to instrument number(s)
× MORTGAGE # CT 902645

Party(ies) (Set out Status or Interest)
Name(s)

MARKET BLOCK TORONTO PROPERTIES LTD.,

(Assignor)

Signature(s)   *[signature]* Per: Andrew M. Clarke, President

I have authority to bind the corporation.

Date of Signature Y M D
1987 09 30

Address for Service   116 Yorkville Avenue, Toronto, Ontario M5R 1C2

Party(ies) (Set out Status or Interest)
Name(s)

THE PRUDENTIAL INSURANCE COMPANY OF
AMERICA, BY ITS SOLICITORS, WOOLLEY,
DALE & DINGWALL

Signature(s)   WOOLLEY, DALE & DINGWALL
Per: Phillip P. Macdonald

Date of Signature Y M D
1987 09 30

Address for Service   200 Consilium Place, Scarborough, Ontario M1H 3E6 Attn: Real Estate Investment Office

Municipal Address of Property
41, 43 and 45 Front
Street East
Toronto, Ontario

(15) Document Prepared by:
Phillip P. Macdonald
Woolley, Dale & Dingwall
P.O. Box 65
Toronto-Dominion Centre
Toronto, Ontario M5K 1E7

Fees and Tax
Registration Fee $11.5?

FOR OFFICE USE ONLY

Royal   Gendarmerie
Canadian   royale
Mounted   du
Police   Canada

Sgt. M.J. Thomson
NCO i/c Central Intake & Admin. Support,
Greater Toronto Area Commercial Crime Section
2755 Highpoint Drive,
Milton, Ontario L9T 2X7

Your File   Votre référence

Mr. Anthony Crawford
223 Rebecca Street, Unit 37,
Oakville, Ontario
L6K 3Y2

Our File   Notre référence
2006 - 282851

October 23, 2006

Dear Mr. Crawford

Michael G. Perris 'et al'

This matter has been extensively reviewed, and rereviewed in order to determine the appropriate jurisdictional purview into which this matter should fall. I regret the delay in responding, however, this matter is convoluted and understandably requires careful study.

From the preponderance of information supplied, it would seem that Michael Perris has performed an element of misrepresentation in the sale of unregistered securities to you and your wife and in the obtaining of the subsequent bank loans in your name. If, as suggested, he has performed this same act in other instances, this would, of course, multiply the number of potential alleged criminal acts. As an unlicensed agent and/or dealer, he is further liable to enforcement provisions under the Ontario Securities Act as well as from the Independent Dealers' Association. This could further affect Perris' then-wife, and their mutual company, Mikary Investments Ltd., and potentially make them both liable to criminal prosecution as accomplices, aiding and abetting.

Similarly, Michael R. Emory is subject to the same allegations of potential criminal conduct with the addition of having allegedly uttered one or more forged documents, as well as other potential statutory misconduct. It remains to be determined to what degree the bank manager, Ian Fardoe, has gained from his involvement as a potential alleged co-conspirator. Emory and Perris are subject to review of their ethical conduct in this matter by their respective professional associations. Fardoe is subject to the same by his bank's internal policies. All and sundry are potentially liable to civil litigation.

This matter is deemed to fall within the sole purview of the agency of local jurisdiction, Halton Regional Police Service. Any subsequent misrepresentation or utterances of forged documents by Emory would be the reponsibility of Toronto Police Service. The Ontario Securities Commission and Independent Dealers' Association have jurisdiction in relation to their Provincial Statutes. Under these circumstances, this matter will not be selected by this office for investigation and our interest in this matter will be considered closed.

Canadä

Crawford v. Bank of Montreal, 2009 ONCA 98 (CanLII)

Print: PDF Format
Date: 2009-01-30
Docket: C49171
URL: http://www.canlii.org/en/on/onca/doc/2009/2009onca98/2009onca98.html
Noteup: Search for decisions citing this decision

Reflex Record (related decisions, legislation cited and decisions cited)

CITATION: Crawford v. Bank of Montreal, 2009 ONCA 98
DATE: 20090130
DOCKET: C49171

COURT OF APPEAL FOR ONTARIO

Gillese, MacFarland and LaForme JJ.A.

BETWEEN:

Anthony Crawford also known as Tony Crawford

Defendant (Appellant)

and

Bank of Montreal

Respondent (Plaintiff)

AND BETWEEN:

Anthony Crawford also known as Tony Crawford

Plaintiff by Counterclaim (Appellant)

and

Bank of Montreal, Avalon Securities Corp., and Michael Perris, Mikary Investments Ltd.,
Gordon E. Glenn, John M. Graydon, William Wright, Donald Ivey, Robert Pell, and
Douglas Ferguson

Defendant by Counterclaim (Respondent)

J. Whitehead, for the appellant
Joshua Siegel, for the respondent
Heard: January 30, 2009

On appeal from the order of Justice Harris of the Superior Court of Justice, dated June 27,
2008.

APPEAL BOOK ENDORSEMENT

[1]   We see no error in the decision below. The essence of the defence in this matter is that the
appellant failed to read the loan documentation when he initially took out the loan or at any point in the
following ten-year period when he made payments on the loan. The loan documentation makes it clear
that there is no genuine issue for trial in relation to the Bank of Montreal.

[2]   Accordingly, the appeal is dismissed with costs to the respondent fixed at $6,000, all inclusive.

Financial

Turner seeks eternal vigilance over banks

Richard Wachman

Lord Turner, chairman of the Financial services Authority, calls for strict control over banking sector's exotic activities

Lord Turner, chairman of the Financial Services Authority, warned last night that the financial system faces new risks despite the global regulatory overhaul in the wake of the banking crisis.

His words come amid renewed fears about stability in the eurozone after Moody's cut Portugal's credit rating, and analysts warned the country could follow Greece and Ireland in seeking a bailout.

Speaking at the Cass Business School in London, Turner warned against complacency, saying: "We are deluding ourselves if we think there is any one policy - one silver bullet - which will permanently ensure a more stable system."

Turner called for careful control of shadow banking - the hedge fund, derivatives and private equity industries - to ensure new risks do not emerge outside mainstream banking.

He suggested systemically important firms, the banks dubbed "too big to fail", should be required to hold more capital than new thresholds agreed by the Basel committee on banking supervision.

Turner said: "(We) should identify whether financial activities are shifting to new institutions and markets. If in response to Basel III, credit extension moves to new shadow bank markets and firms, for instance to hedge funds, and within those markets and firms we are aware of bank-like risks, such as high leverage, we need to spot that and if necessary extend the reach of regulation."

The FSA chairman stopped short of calling for the break-up of big banks by ordering them to separate their retail arms from their more risky investment banking operations. But he threw his weight behind a review of the issue by the banking commission, which is due to report in September.

Turner said the commission under Sir John Vickers should not be constrained by any assumption that the "present complex structures of banks always deliver vital social benefits - too often indeed, they reflect the objectives of tax avoidance and regulatory arbitrage." But he added that breaking up large banks might not be a panacea, since risks could also arise from the complex inter-connectedness of many small banks.

Looking at the pitfalls of future regulation of the City, Turner said the pre-crisis delusion was that the financial system was secure because risk was widely spread among scores of financial institutions. That proved to be entirely wrong.

"But the temptation post-crisis is to imagine that if we can only discover and correct the crucial imperfections - the bad incentives and structures - a permanent, more stable financial system can be achieved. It cannot, because financial instability is driven by human myopia and imperfect rationality as well as by poor incentives; and because any financial system will mutate to create new risks."

Turner said the system could be made more stable, but it required a continually evolving regulatory response. "For the very fact of imposing stricter regulations will induce changes, requiring new regulatory responses."

The FSA chairman's speech came after a turbulent day in Europe, with Moody's downgrading Portugal's credit rating to just four notches above "junk".

Dear Ms Crawford:

Re: **Lawyer:**   **Joshua Siegel**
      Complainant: Anthony Crawford
      Case No.:   **2009-72179**   March 18, 2010

I am writing to follow up on your letter dated February 5 and 13, 2010 and enclosures to Malcolm Heins – Chief Executive Officer, of the Law Society of Upper Canada (CEO) regarding your concerns about Mr. Siegel.

Your letter was forwarded to me in my capacity as Senior Counsel and Assistant Manager of the Complaints Resolution Department because it relates to a closed complaints file. In response to your request, I have reviewed and considered the information you provided as well as the closed complaints file.

The Law Society received a complaint on January 21, 2009 from your spouse Anthony Crawford. Mr. Crawford alleged that Mr. Siegel misled the Court by denying the existence of a second promissory note and the existence of another action involving you and Mr. Crawford. As you know the case was assigned to M. Joanne MacMillan, Complaints Resolution Counsel. By letter dated December 4, 2009 Ms MacMillan provided you with a summary of the evidence obtained during the investigation and also informed you of the outcome. I note that you did not request a review by the Complaints Resolution Commissioner.

Your recent correspondence raised issues already mentioned in your initial complaint and addressed in the original investigation. The other concerns you raised include:

- legal fees;
- clearing Writ No.: 09-0000025;
- removal of a Writ of Execution relating to BMO proceeding;
- Mr. Siegal's refusal to produce a "Mutual release" signed by BMO;
- Mr. Siegel's involvement on a Motion for Particulars;
- BMO's tactics to "win court order for $80,000" with threatening letters and phone calls for money plus coercion for a signature on mutual release has been too onerous to survive unscathed";
- your husband's health;
- threatening phone calls, demands for money, and seizure of property.

You also indicated in your e-mail that your "priority is that he remove paid Writs for Debt without trial in the case of BMO v Anthony Crawford 1678/02".

Your concerns arose in the context of ongoing court proceedings. Also, your request for the removal of the writs relates directly to those proceedings. The Court is the appropriate forum for addressing them. The Law Society cannot intervene in, make legal findings in, change the results of, or provide legal advice about your legal matter. The Court controls its own process.

Also, Mr. Siegel has a professional obligation to act in the best interest of his client. He receives instructions from his client and provides the legal advice he believes to be in the best interest of his client subject to his professional and legal obligations as an officer of the Court. In doing so you may not always agree with the strategies he adopts and legal advice he provides to his client. He does not require your approval as to the manner in which he represents his client.

Please note also that the Law Society regulates lawyers and paralegals in the public interest. According to our records Mr. Downe is not a licensee of the Law Society.

Yours truly,

They can rob you blind — and it's legal

ROB LAMBERTI
Toronto Sun

Tony Crawford thought he was investing in his retirement golden egg.

Instead, his dreams were scrambled when a bank called demanding payment for a loan he didn't know existed.

What's worse, Crawford said, is that the system that ultimately cost him his house — sold to cover legal fees fighting a lawsuit filed by a bank demanding payment — is legal.

Crawford said he was stung for $110,000 on a loan issued by a bank he doesn't have an account with. The loan was apparently granted based on information in an affidavit filed by a third party.

He said he thought he had been investing in a retirement plan, but unknown to him the monthly payments he made were used to cover monthly loan payments on a loan taken out by his financial adviser through a lawyer.

The tied loans scheme is complex but ultimately legal and leaves unsuspecting investors on the hook for huge amounts in loans they didn't know existed.

The Oakville man wants some changes to banking laws to prevent the affidavit-backed loans, which he calls "Sitting Duck Loans."

"Basically, that rule ... where any affidavit will do, can draw people into debt ... and put the bank into position where they say they have information which they can trust and it can issue a loan to anybody because the credit is paid by somebody else."

"You think you're investing," Crawford said. "Ten years later, the bank calls in the loan and want the full amount plus interest."

The Canadian Bankers Association had no comment.

CRAWFORD
Ripped off

Crawford thought his accountant was investing in real estate.

The bank has sued Crawford for payment and he has filed a counterclaim saying he had no knowledge of the loan. Neither case has been proven in court.

The investment scheme involved 300 people and $22 million, Crawford said. He said 15 other burned investors are considering launching a class action suit against the bank but are waiting to see what happens with Crawford's counter-suit against the bank.

Last weekend, Crawford launched a petition at the Ontario NDP convention, where he garnered 431 signatures calling for an investigation into the loans practice.